Treasures of the Taylorian
Series Three: Cultural Memory
Volume 9

German in the World

Exhibition Catalogue for the
Association for German Studies
Conference 2025

Edited by Henrike Lähnemann
and Christina Ostermann

Series Editor: Henrike Lähnemann
Taylor Institution Library, Oxford, 2025

Taylor Institution Library
St Giles, Oxford, OX1 3NA

http://editions.mml.ox.ac.uk

© 2025 The Authors

Some rights are reserved. This book is made available under the Creative Commons Attribution-Non-Commercial-No Derivative Works 4.0 International (CC BY 4.0). This license allows for copying any part of the work for personal and non-commercial use, providing author attribution is clearly stated.

Digital downloads for this edition are available at
https://historyofthebook.mml.ox.ac.uk
They include a pdf eBook of the text.

Every effort has been made to trace copyright holders and to obtain their permission for the use of copyright material within this text. If you believe you hold copyright of any of the material and we have not requested your permission, please contact the Taylor Institution Library <tay-enquiries@bodleian.ox.ac.uk>.

Typesetting by Henrike Lähnemann
Cover design by Emma Huber
Cover image photograph Henrike Lähnemann

ISBN 978-1-0686058-6-4

Printed in the United Kingdom and United States by Lightning Source for Taylor Institution Library

Table of Contents

Preface
Henrike Lähnemann v

German(s) at Oxford. The Taylorian in the 19th Century
Christina Ostermann 1

Black. German. Womxn
Natasha A. Kelly / Santhia Velasco Kittlaus 15

The Worlds of German Song. Programme Notes for the Recital
Anhad Arora 31

Exhibition Catalogue 'German in the World' 51
    Case 1: German in the World. Introduction 52
    Case 2: *West-Eastern Divan* & *Ringparabel* 58
    Case 3: German in Oxford 64
    Case 4: The *Nibelungenlied* as German World 70
    Case 5: Natasha A. Kelly 73

The statues above the entrance to the Taylorian
Photograph Henrike Lähnemann

Henrike Lähnemann
Preface

The exhibition 'German in the World' accompanies the 2025 Association for German Studies conference at the University of Oxford. Both build on the founding principles of the Taylor Institution Library: to chart the development of 'Nationalliteratur' in the context of 'Weltliteratur', to look at how global perspectives have shaped German literature, and to make visible how in turn German-language poetry, pamphlets, and philosophy have spread across the globe.

The Taylorian itself was founded in the 19th century, at the time of establishing the 'canon' of German literature, dedicated to making texts in their original form available to scholars and students, starting with incunables and going to the newest contemporary literature. The four figures standing proud over the St Giles entrance of the building represent Italian, French, German, and Spanish literature as a collective of women: enlightening, scattering a cornucopia, thinking, and fighting.

This volume is itself a cornucopia of different genres and forms approaching the topic of German in the world; and the world represented within German literature. The opening essay by Christina Ostermann explores the early history of the Taylorian, the venue for the exhibition, and shows how the interests of German academics and librarians (Case 3) shaped its holdings in ways that remain influential even today, as visible in the most recent publications (Case 1).

Following it, the text by Natasha A. Kelly, this year's President's Guest at the AGS, consists of a translation of three chapters of her influential book 'Schwarz. Weiblich. Deutsch', which was done in conversation with Santhia Velasco Kittlaus who prefaced it and also curated Case 5.

Anhad Arora wrote the next chapter as programme notes for the recital at the opening of the exhibition which features German *Lieder* – one of the main exports of German literature but also in itself heavily influenced by other cultures and languages. He also curated Case 2, which features the *West-östlicher Divan* as a prime example of such an exchange.

At the end of the volume stands the catalogue for the exhibition itself, which builds on the Taylorian collection, supplemented by Bodleian holdings and private loans from Oxford colleagues. In addition to the topics of German in Oxford, the *Divan*, and the work of Natasha A. Kelly, there is a special focus on the *Nibelungenlied* as a German world unto itself. The medieval epic has formed the backbone of lecturing since the beginning of German Studies in Oxford. The otherness of its world still holds a fascination for German authors today, as the new interpretation of it by Ulrike Draesner shows (Case 4). Draesner will be a guest at the 28th Anglo-German Colloquium, the biennial meeting of German medievalists, which will follow on directly after the AGS, also taking place at the Taylorian.

We are grateful to all who helped make this exhibition and catalogue happen; Emma Huber and the other librarians at the Taylorian; colleagues from across the UK, Ireland, Germany, and beyond; and the cultural and political institutions whose support keeps the subject alive – with a special mention to the Austrian Embassy and the Austrian Cultural Forum who help to celebrate the opening of the exhibition with Austrian wine.

May *German in the World* continue to flourish!

Oxford, August 2025
Henrike Lähnemann for the organisers and authors

Christina Ostermann
German(s) at Oxford
The Taylorian in the 19th Century

The Taylorian before the extension of 1932. c1880s,
Oxford, Bodleian Libraries, University Archives, TL 5/11

In central Oxford, at the corner of St Giles and Beaumont Street, stands a stately building, most notably featuring four statues of women high on pillars: the Taylor Institution (or Taylorian for short). Today, students, staff, locals, and tourists alike regard it as an impressive landmark – yet in its early days, the building stirred controversy. Professor Friedrich Max Müller, the Institution's second Professor of European Languages, later recalled:

> I still remember the outcry against the Taylor Institution, the only Palladian building at Oxford, and yet everybody has now grown reconciled to it, and even Ruskin lectured in it, which he would not have done, if he had disapproved of its architecture.[1]

Yet there was method in this apparent madness of adorning central Victorian Oxford with a building seemingly so out of place: the four statues represent the four languages central to this Institution – from left to right, Italian, French, German and Spanish. Founded in the mid-nineteenth century, the Taylor Institution Library was established to promote the study of modern European languages, particularly those spoken in countries maintaining diplomatic or commercial relations with Britain.[2] German was, in fact, central to the Taylorian from the outset, and in more than one respect.

In its first decades, two German-born philologists played a key role in shaping the character and collections of the Library: the above-quoted Friedrich Max Müller, second Professor of Modern European Languages (1854–68) and later first Professor of Comparative Philology (1868–1900), and Heinrich Krebs, the Institution's second Librarian (1871–1921). Max Müller's intellectual interests guided the library's acquisition policy, while Krebs was responsible for implementing it. Their work left a lasting mark on the Taylor Institution that endures to this day.

This paper explores the early history of the Taylorian with a particular focus on these two Germans most closely associated with the library's formative years. I will begin by outlining the major milestones in the early history of the Taylor Institution Library, tracing

---

[1] John Ruskin, Oxford's first Slade Professor of Fine Art "would never lecture in the Indian Institute, and wrote me a letter sadly reproving me for causing Broad Street to be defaced by such a building, when I had had absolutely nothing to do with it", Friedrich Max Müller, *My Autobiography. A Fragment* (Longmans, Green, 1901), p. 216; online.

[2] See Jill Hughes's blog post on the website of the Bodleian Library.

its emergence from a contested bequest to its formal establishment and first decades of operation.³ I will then turn to brief portraits of Friedrich Max Müller and Heinrich Krebs, and also Krebs's daughter Luisa, whose autobiography *The Chronicle of Wisa Dingeldey by Herself* offers a glimpse into daily life at the library towards the end of the nineteenth century.⁴

Foundation and Early Years of the Taylorian

The development of the Taylor Institution Library in the 19th century unfolded over several decades. The timeline below outlines key moments in the foundation and early years of the library. Highlighting milestones from 1835 through to 1900, this chronology provides the structural backdrop against which the later contributions of Friedrich Max Müller and Heinrich Krebs can be more fully understood.⁵

> 1835: Following a long legal dispute, the University of Oxford receives £65,000 from the estate of architect Sir Robert Taylor (1714–88). Taylor intended the money to be used as the financial basis for the establishment of an institution dedicated to the promotion of European languages and literature.

---

³ This paper focuses on the history of the Taylorian in the 19th century. For a broader account of German Studies at Oxford from the 19th century to the present day – with a particular focus on the 20th century – see Ritchie Robertson, 'German Studies at Oxford: Past and Future', Oxford German Studies, 50.4 (2022), 398–405.

⁴ *Luisa Hewitt, The Girl Who Lived in the Library*, ed. by Christina Ostermann (Treasures of the Taylorian: Series 2: Writers in Residence, vol. 5), 2025.

⁵ The timeline draws on the work of Jill Hughes, former German Subject Librarian at the Taylorian; see her blog post mentioned in fn. 2 as well as her entry on the Taylor Institution Library in *Handbuch der historischen Buchbestände in Deutschland*, ed. by Bernhard Fabian (Olms Neue Medien, 2003), online. Another valuable source was the introduction to the Taylorian on the Oxford University Archives website (author unspecified, though its style and content suggest Jill Hughes).

1839: Convocation appoints fourteen delegates to select plans for the planned institution and an accompanying art gallery (future Ashmolean Museum).[6]

1841: Construction for the building begins on Beaumont Street under the supervision of architect Charles Robert Cockerell.

1844: The construction of the building is completed.

1845: The first regulations for the planned institution are approved by Convocation and nine Curators are appointed for its governance.

1847: A statute establishing the Taylor Institution Library as a centre for the teaching of modern languages (excluding English) is passed.
John Macray is appointed the Institution's first Librarian.

1848: Friedrich Heinrich Trithen, a Swiss-born Sanskrit scholar, is appointed the Institution's first Professor of Modern European Languages.

1849: The Taylor Institution Library officially opens.

1850: Trithen falls ill and Friedrich Max Müller is subsequently appointed Deputy Professor at the age of 27.

1854: Trithen dies.
Max Müller is appointed Professor of Modern European Languages.

1868: The chair of Modern European Languages is abolished as Max Müller becomes Oxford's first Professor of Comparative Philology.

1871: Heinrich Krebs succeeds John Macray as the Institution's second librarian, serving until 1921.

---

[6] The latter was not paid with money from Taylor's bequest, but a separate legacy established by Sir Francis Randolph in 1796.

1875: Max Müller resigns from his professorship at the Taylorian.

1876: Oxford University persuades Max Müller to remain at the Institution, granting his wish to be released from all his duties, including teaching, so that he could focus on his research in Sanskrit.

1880/81:[7] Krebs's daughter Luisa Hewitt, née Krebs, is born.

1885: Krebs's wife – Luisa's mother – dies and Luisa is raised by her father alone. She grows up in the Taylor Institution where the family lives in the Librarian's flat in the basement. Her autobiography *The Life of Wisa Dingeldey by Herself*, written in 1930/31 and published by the Taylor Institution in 2025, offers a personal account of this childhood in the library at the end of the 19th century.

1900: Max Müller dies.

Friedrich Max Müller

The story of the Taylor Institution Library cannot be told without Friedrich Max Müller (in England known as 'Max Müller'), one of the most prominent scholars of the 19th century.[8] Max Müller's work on Sanskrit, religion and philology attracted considerable attention and his lectures on topics such as *The Science of Religion*, *The History of German Literature*, and the *Nibelungenlied* found a wide audience.[9]

---

[7] The exact year of Luisa Krebs's birth (later Luisa Hewitt) is not documented, but her autobiography points towards 1880/81.

[8] John R. Davis and Angus Nicholls, 'Friedrich Max Müller: The Career and Intellectual Trajectory of a German Philologist in Victorian Britain', *Publications of the English Goethe Society*, 85.2–3 (2016), 67–97. Lourens P. van den Bosch, *Friedrich Max Müller. A Life Devoted to Humanities* (E. J. Brill, 2002).

[9] The Taylorian holds several of Max Müller's lecture notes, see the exhibition case 4 for the *Nibelungenlied* lectures. Another example are his *Four Lectures on Science of Religion* delivered in 1870 (MS 8° E 10 B). They were later published by Longman, London in 1873. A digital version of this edition is available via Google Books.

'Frederick Maximilian Müller, LL D' in Vanity Fair, 6 February 1875
Taylorian, uncatalogued. Photograph Christina Ostermann

A *Vanity Fair* article on him by Thomas Gibson Bowles praised him as an internationally leading scholar and concluded: "Max Müller, although he has become very English, has not ceased to be intensely German. [...] He is regarded and has been used as the apostle and unavowed Ambassador of Prussia in England among the extra-official personages".[10] Largely forgotten by the general public today, his work lives on in scholarly circles through his edition of the *Rigveda*, a sacred text of Hinduism and one of the oldest surviving religious works in the world, while his name endures in the Goethe Institutes in India, which are known as Max Müller Bhavans.

A German native of Dessau and the son of the poet Wilhelm Müller – best known for writing the lyrics to two of Franz Schubert's song cycles – Max Müller was raised by a single mother after his father's early death, making a professorship at Oxford seem an unlikely prospect. Looking back on his career at the end of his life, he reflected:

> For me to go to Oxford to get a fellowship or professorship would have seemed about as absurd as going to Rome to become a Cardinal or a Pope; [...] no one was more surprised than myself when I was asked to act as deputy, and then as full Taylorian Professor; [...] My ambition had never soared so high. I was thinking of returning to Leipzig as a Privat-docent, to rise afterwards to an extraordinary and, if all went well, to an ordinary professorship.[11]

In his autobiography, Max Müller portrays himself as entirely focused on his academic interests, wholly indifferent to career politics, and fully reliant on his influential friends. The truthfulness of this self-image may be questioned – indeed, even his son does so in his foreword to his father's autobiography[12] – yet it is undeniable that his social environment benefited him. His mother, Adelheid Müller (née

---

[10] Vanity Fair, 6 February 1875, among the 'Men of the Day' (No. XCVIII), p. 75.
[11] Max Müller, *Autobiography*, p. 22.
[12] Max Müller's son William Grenfell Max Müller writes: 'The real secret of his [Max Müller's] success lay not in his friends, but in himself', Max Müller, *Autobiography*, p. viii.

Basedow), came from a noble family with members in powerful positions: her father, Ludwig Basedow, served as *Regierungspräsident* (President of the Regional Government) in Dessau and her grandfather, Johann Bernhard Basedow, was a well-known educational reformer. This family background gave Max Müller access to influential circles from his earliest years. As an adult, he continued to socialise with some of the most distinguished academics of his time. In March 1845, he recorded in his diary: 'My stay in Berlin is over; I have made many and influential friends there – Schelling, Rückert, Humboldt, Bopp, Jacobi, Mendelssohn.'[13] Roughly a decade later, Alexander von Humboldt wrote a letter in support of Max Müller's appointment to the Taylorian professorship; the Prussian diplomat Christian Karl Josias von Bunsen, one of Max Müller's strongest sponsors, added his endorsement.[14]

Friedrich Max Müller liked to think of himself as a product of his environment, shaped by his friendships and his intellectual milieu. The Taylor Institution Library, in turn, stands as a product of Max Müller himself. His personal interests, particularly Luther and the Reformation, influenced the library's holdings and continue to do so to this day.[15] His personal admiration for Martin Luther and his conviction that Oxford in the 19th century needed a 'Reformation 2.0', shaped the Taylorian's acquisition policy in decisive ways. Tracing the Library's collection of 400 Reformation pamphlets back through time, Max Müller's influence becomes clear: from early chance purchases in 1868, to a major acquisition drive in the 1870s for which he secured dedicated funding, to later additions under the Finch Fund in the 20th century, when Max Müller was no longer alive. His

---

[13] See *The Life and Letters of the Right Honourable Friedrich Max Müller*, ed. by his wife (2 volumes). London, New York and Bombay 1902, vol. i, p. 30.
[14] See *Life and Letters*, vol. i, p. 146.
[15] Christina Ostermann and Henrike Lähnemann, 'Friedrich Max Müller and the Acquisition of Reformation Pamphlets at the Taylor Institution Library', *Forum for Modern Language Studies. Special Issue: Migration Collections: Translocation Research in Libraries and Archives, 1850–2025*, ed. by Sophia Buck and Stefanie Hundehege (forthcoming 2026).

roles at the Institution as professor, member of the operational Library Committee, and a governing Curator enabled him to promote Luther's writings as scholarly resources that remain central to German teaching at Oxford today.

Gravestone of Friedrich Max Müller (1823–1900) in Holywell Cemetery, Oxford.
'The right honourable Frederick Max Müller'
'Fellow of All Soul's College, for fifty years professor in this university, born at Dessau 6 Dec 1823, died at Oxford 28 October 1900'.
He is buried together with his wife Georgina Adelaide, their son William and William's wife Wanda Maria. Photograph Christina Ostermann

10 *Christina Ostermann*

Heinrich Krebs and Luisa Hewitt

Heinrich Krebs and his daughter Luisa Hewitt, née Krebs, c. 1895
Photograph Christina Ostermann

While Max Müller shaped the Taylorian's vision, it was the Librarian who put that vision into practice – first John Macray and, from 1871, Henrich Krebs. The job advertisement published after John Macray's retirement describes the Librarian's duties as follows:[16]

---

[16] TL 3/55/1 Correspondence of the Librarian, mainly with publishers and booksellers, relating to the acquisitions of books, with some applications to read and borrow, and testimonials for borrowers. 1859-1941.

The Librarian is appointed and removable by the Curators, who have also power to regulate his duties from time to time at their discretion.

The Library is open at hours fixed from time to time by the Curators. The time now required amounts to six hours a day, during which the Librarian must be present. It is open on all week days except Good Friday, a week at Christmas and a month in Long Vacation.

New Catalogues will have to be made, and the task of making them will form part of the Librarian's duties. The stipend is to begin with £120 per annum, but it may be raised at the discretion of the Curators to £150. There is a residence on the premises which the Librarian may occupy by permission of the Curators. No person above 40 years of age will be considered eligible.

A competent knowledge of French and German will be required from applicants. Testimonials may be sent under cover to the Library Committee, Taylor Institution, Oxford.

H. G. LIDDEL, Vice-Chancellor
TAYLOR INSTITUTION, March 11, 1871

Heinrich Krebs, a native of Darmstadt who had previously worked as a private tutor in Switzerland and England, was the successful candidate. He served as Librarian for half a century – and thus for most of Müller's tenure – implementing the professor's acquisition policy. In her edition of Max Müller's letters, his widow Georgina Adelaide Müller underlined Krebs's value to her husband, particularly in his later years:

> Mention should be made of the constant help Max Müller received in these later years from Dr. Krebs, the Librarian of the Taylor Institution. He said himself that he never appealed to him in vain.[17]

---

[17] *Life and Letters*, vol 2, p. 383. 1899, Chapter XXXIV – editorial note.

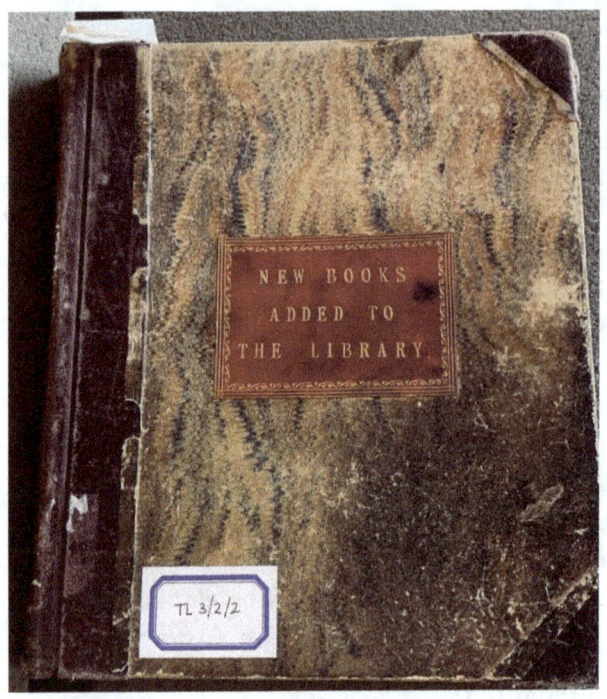

Registers of additions to the Library (accession registers). 1871-77 University Archives, TL 3/2/2. Photograph Christina Ostermann

Similar praise came from the historian Charles Firth:

> Dr. Krebs rearranged and catalogued the whole Library, two tasks which his predecessor had failed to perform to the satisfaction of the Curators. He was accurate, scholarly, and infinitely industrious, possessed an exact knowledge of the contents of the collection under his charge, and kept himself extremely well informed about new publications dealing with language or literature. A reader studying any particular subject found the Librarian a constant helper; he would call attention to new books on it, or to articles which had recently appeared in learned periodicals.[18]

---

[18] Charles Firth, *Modern Languages at Oxford 1724–1929* (Oxford University Press, Humphrey Milford, 1929).

The most vivid portrait of Krebs is provided by his daughter Luisa, who lived with him in the basement of the Taylorian. In her autobiography *The Chronicle of Wisa Dingeldey by Herself*, Luisa recalls this childhood in the Taylorian. What might at first seem rather splendid – and Luisa's friends reportedly did envy her childhood in this grand building – was far from idyllic. The basement rooms were damp and dark, and her father was a man of peculiar habits and strict routines, both in his work and private life:[19]

According to Luisa, her father's day followed a invariable pattern: He rose early, dressed formally, took a morning walk, and was in the Library punctually for the start of opening hours at 11 a.m. He would then focus on his duties, be it cataloguing new books and periodicals, submitting others on approval to the Library Committee, setting aside volumes for the binder and returning them to the shelves, or advising readers on relevant works. He knew his collection inside out and was diligent in reclaiming overdue books. Luisa Hewitt recalls a legendary episode in which her father wrote to a recently deceased borrower: 'Sir, since you can no longer have any possible use for the copy of ..., please to return it at once to the library.'

The reading room was seldom busy, allowing Krebs time for his own studies. After closing the library at 5 p.m., he often stayed on to complete small tasks before taking his evening walk. His evenings were spent reading, sometimes, on better days, with his cat curled up on his knees. Krebs was a singular figure: meticulous, self-disciplined, and eccentric, famously wearing two hats and insisting on adhering to exactly the same weekly menu for decades. His life-long service, deep knowledge of the collections, and unwavering dedication to their care left an enduring mark on the Taylorian, to which the library owes much of its character today. The acquisitions registers he compiled as well as his memoranda books now held in the Taylorian Archive bear witness to this.

---

[19] Luisa Hewitt, *The Girl Who Lived in the Library*, Chapter 37: My Father.

Memoranda book of the librarian Heinrich Krebs with correspondence, pamphlets, and a report to the Curators about books missing from the Finch Collection University Archives, TL 3/27/1. Photograph Christina Ostermann

Natasha A. Kelly & Santhia Velasco Kittlaus
Black. German. Womxn.
Why Feminism Must Demand More Than Gender Equality

Translated from the original German by the author Natasha A. Kelly, with a prologue and editorial refinement by Santhia Velasco Kittlaus

Prologue

Have you ever been asked for directions by a Black person? Take a moment to really consider that question. Take it with you on your walks. I began to notice, as someone who first learned to see the world through a German lens and then walked into the world with this experience, that, when lost, my Black friends would often wait. They would let four, five white people pass, to ask the next Black person along the path for directions. This observation taught me that I can hide my own intersectionality behind my white, German identity whenever it feels safe. I learned that encounters with white people like me in unfamiliar places do not feel safe for Black people.

From Natasha A. Kelly's *Schwarz. Deutsch. Weiblich* I learned to understand why that is. In the following chapter from the book, which is published here in English for the first time, one encounters an elderly white woman in a German neighbourhood who mutters meanly towards a Black little girl happily on her way to buy some ice-cream, only to scare the child back into the house. Passages like this felt to me as though a veil had been lifted from my memory and enabled me to see my friend's walks with me as theirs, not mine. I understood that they must have walked past so many white people on their life's way who deeply hurt and perhaps even endangered them that there really are not enough reasons why one would trust a white stranger as a Black person. As white people in this world, we have yet to do better to change the embodied experiences of the Black futures.

Natasha A. Kelly's Afrofuturist works show the potential that lies ahead. In her imagination lies a lesson, like a gift. As her reader, I learned to think from a perspective that I was never taught to see. Sometimes, the narrative voice comes as harsh, always poetic, and necessary reminder of one's own whiteness, a reminder of Germany's still flourishing racism, and how we continue to think through history with its legacies, yet unable to see futures like the ones Kelly dares to think. Some of her experiences are familiar, depending on who we are as readers, for there are injustices we share. Perhaps the most meaningful aspect of reading Natasha A. Kelly is to understand intersectionality as something that speaks to the experiences of most of us. In our shared vulnerability, we learn to understand what makes us vulnerable from the most vulnerable: Black womxn. Womxn like Sojourner Truth. Kimberlé Williams Crenshaw. Mary Seacole. Queen Nanny. Alice Walker. All of which Natasha A. Kelly introduces, passing on their stories to the present – as educators, like herself.

Screenshot from the film 'Milli's Awakening' (2018)
Credits: Anh Trieu / Henning Fehr / Philipp Rühr

1. "Ain't I a Woman?"

In my youth, I often asked myself whether I was a 'real' woman or if I could ever become one.
Not because I rejected or struggled with the gender assigned to me at birth, but because I rarely saw myself reflected in the narrow, homogeneous category of 'woman' presented to me. I often felt that something was wrong with me. I did not fit the dominant white ideals of femininity, nor beauty. My womanhood was rarely acknowledged, let alone affirmed.

In a speech Black US-American freedom fighter Sojourner Truth once said: "The man says women must be helped into carriages, and lifted over ditches, and given the best place everywhere. But no one ever helps me into a carriage, or over a mud puddle, or gives me the best place. Ain't I a woman?"

Sojourner Truth was born around 1797 in Ulster County, New York, into slavery. The exact date is unknown. After escaping enslavement, she became one of the most powerful voices of her time, speaking out against multiple forms of discrimination as early as the mid-19th century. Although she could neither read nor write, she travelled across the United States, addressing the social and political conditions of women in general and Black women in particular. At the 1851 Women's Rights Convention in Akron, Ohio, she drew on her lived experience to lay the groundwork for a form of intersectional critique that continues to resonate today.

The version of Sojourner Truth's speech available to me was transcribed in 1858 by a white woman named Frances Gage. Although her phrasing reproduces racist stereotypes, Sojourner Truth's words still spoke directly to my soul. She made it unmistakably clear that womanhood is not a monolith and that feminism must account for the many differences among women. Long before the term intersectionality existed, she understood that, unlike white women, she faced both racism and sexism – simultaneously.

However, it took until 1989 for Black US-American legal scholar Kimberlé Williams Crenshaw to introduce 'intersectionality' as a framework to make these overlapping forms of discrimination visible.

Kimberlé Williams Crenshaw, born in 1959 in Canton, Ohio, the daughter of two Black US-American educators, dreamed from a young age of becoming a lawyer – and did. Before joining the faculty at UCLA in 1986, she worked as a courtroom attorney. Through her legal practice and academic research, she came to see how deeply embedded racism remained in the U.S. legal system – even after the passage of the Civil Rights Act. Drawing on Critical Race Theory, she developed intersectionality as a lens to analyze how systems of oppression interact.

Crenshaw's work was rooted in a specific legal case, DeGraffenreid v. General Motors (1976), in which five Black women sued their employer for structural discrimination. They had been the last to be hired and the first to be fired. The court dismissed their claim, arguing that because white women had not been fired, it could not be sexism; and because Black men had not been fired, it could not be racism. What the court failed to grasp was that the women were dismissed precisely because of their specific social position. As Black Women, they were subjected to both racism and sexism, simultaneously. Ironically, it was this failed lawsuit that allowed Crenshaw to show how discrimination is not additive but intersectional, arising from the combined effects of multiple systems of oppression.

In recent years, intersectionality has become something of a buzzword in German-speaking spaces. It now appears across academia, politics, art, and culture. But rarely is it connected to its roots in Black feminist thought. However, it is undeniable that Sojourner Truth stands among the earliest voices in Black feminist history to call for what we now describe as intersectional justice. She denounced white women for their racism, and both white and Black men for the sexism she endured. And she fought for the rights of Black women and for women's suffrage for all.

Although time and distance separated me from Sojourner Truth, I had experiences similar to hers, ones I was unable to name for a long time. To most white men, I did not exist as a full human being. And white women rarely held back their racism toward me. As a result, I found it difficult to fully align myself with their feminist struggles. To this day, I struggle to understand why they continue to define womanhood solely from their own white perspective while expecting all other women to conform to it.

However, Sojourner Truth's identity was far more complex than it may appear at first glance. She was not only Black and a woman; she also lived with a physical disability, a fact that is rarely discussed. After an accident in the Dumont household, where she had been forced to work, her right hand was left permanently damaged. In her public appearances and visual portrayals, Sojourner Truth often redirected attention away from her disability and toward her Black womanhood, at times even by exposing her breasts in protest. In doing so, she used her sexual presence to challenge the way she was seen, actively shaping her own image and drawing focus away from her impairment.

With this in mind, I want to emphasize that even within Black feminist contexts, it is essential not to focus solely on our own experiences of discrimination. We must also address forms of oppression that do not affect us personally and may not be immediately visible. More broadly, we must resist separating systems of oppression and instead examine how they are interconnected and mutually reinforcing.

Today, there may be no horse-drawn carriages like in Sojourner Truth's time but metaphorically speaking, no one held the door open for me neither. No red carpet was rolled out. And the way I was raised, I did not expect one. My mother taught me early on to open the door myself, if I wanted to enter a room. Still, without role models I could identify with, that was not easy.

As a child, I did not know any Black women outside of my family. Women who looked like my mother, my sisters, or me were nowhere to be found in 1980s Germany – not on television, not on the streets, and certainly not in the small northern town where I grew up. Wherever I went, I was surrounded by white women. My friends and their mothers were white. My teachers were white. The princesses in my fairy tale books? All white. And not all of these white women left a positive impression.

There is one encounter I remember vividly. I was a little girl when I found a 20-pfennig coin while tidying up. Back then, that was enough to buy a scoop of ice cream.
So I decided to sneak out without telling my mother and head to the ice cream shop around the corner. I closed the apartment door behind me as quietly as I could, hoping she would not hear me. My excitement must have been written all over my face. I rushed down the stairs, bounding toward the street. But I would not get far.

An elderly white woman stopped me by raising her cane and muttering something I could not understand at the time. She scared me. Her skin wrinkled so deeply as she spoke that it hid her eyes, yet somehow she still managed to look straight at me. And that look pierced right through me. I turned on my heel and ran, as fast as my flip-flops could carry me, back inside and up the stairs. The ice cream was forgotten.

I had looked hatred in the face. It had starred straight back. And from that day on, it never left me. To this day, I do not know, what that old woman was trying to say. What I do know is that she stirred something in me, a feeling that stayed with me for years. In my child's mind, she became the evil witch from Hansel and Gretel or Snow White, a living version of Cinderella's wicked stepmother. From then on, three words shaped the way I saw white women: *old*, *ugly*, and *mean*. I had learned at an early age that Black and white women were fundamentally different. And I knew one thing for sure: I did not want to grow up to become someone who frightened children.

What I did not understand at the time was that, as a Black woman, I would one day come to embody a very different kind of fear, one that white women would never have to carry. The centuries-old stereotype that Black women are angry, aggressive, and dangerous would eventually be projected onto me, too. And there would be no way to stop it.

2. The Gateway to the White World

Compared to many other stories of flight and displacement, my migration story is short but still very painful in its own way. Much has already been written about the presence of the U.S. military in southern Germany after World War II. Politically, the US-American armed forces played a central role in the history of Black people in Germany; a legacy undeniably shaped by U.S. imperialism and the Americanization of the West. Less well known, however, is that the British army, which was stationed in northern Germany, also included many Black soldiers from the formerly colonized Caribbean and Pacific islands, as well as from various African nations.

Before I even understood what the 'world' was or how I would need to navigate it, both literally and strategically, my family moved after my mother married a white Englishman. We left East London and relocated to a British military base in northern Germany, where my stepfather was stationed. Isolated from the rest of the country and surrounded by barren fields, we lived among other British families, shopped in British supermarkets, went to British cinemas, and attended a British school. As a child, I believed we were still in Britain until a few years later, when my mother told us children that our stepfather would not be coming home and that we would be moving – again. I did not understand what that meant exactly. I only remember the sudden feeling of emptinesss, a feeling that has stayed with me ever since.

The war between Argentina and the United Kingdom over the Falkland Islands, which lasted from April to June 1982, not only ushered in democracy in Argentina, but also tore through my family like a fault line. My stepfather was sent to fight, but he never returned. The few memories I have of him have faded over the years, but I try to preserve them as best I can.

Since my mother was not a soldier herself, she had no choice but to leave the military. But she did not want to return to Thatcher's Britain. As a Black single mother of four, she feared she would not survive the racism entrenched in the politics of the so-called 'Iron Lady'. So she packed our belongings, took us by the hand, and led us through the gates of the base and into a new life.

With a single step, we left behind the multicultural bubble of the military base and entered Germany. I looked around and saw the world turn white – whiter than ever before. And this expansive whiteness seemed to be a natural fact.

What had been erased, however, were the countless traces of Black people in Germany, especially Black German women, whose presence can be traced back as far as the 17th century. Germany's colonial history had simply been swept under the rug. Later, I would often hear people around me say that "the British were much worse", referring to European colonialism in general, as if to downplay Germany's own historical guilt. Many believed that Germany had already atoned for its crimes through its reckoning with National Socialism. They saw no need to dig deeper into older wounds, let alone confront the histories that came before the Nazis.

What they ignored was the fact that, following the loss of Germany's colonies after World War I, Black people were repeatedly expelled from the country. Their stories were buried under a collective silence that allowed the racism inherited from colonialism, which later fueled Nazi genocide, to remain dormant, but fully intact.

And so, my life was marked early on by European expansionism and white supremacy. Born in London, a child of British imperialism, it did not take long before I would also experience, first-hand, the ongoing legacy of German colonialism and its entanglement with National Socialism.

One day, I was playing with my sisters on the street in front of our new apartment. There were five of us living in a two-room flat, so we kids spent most of our time outside. It was there that I first encountered the elderly white woman with the deep facial wrinkles. From that moment on, I was always alert, never really feeling completely safe.

Across the street stood a supermarket that saw steady foot traffic. But instead of going about their business, white people would stop in their tracks, grocery bags in hand, and stare at us as if we were animals roaming free. For many in that village, we were the first Black children they had ever seen. We were a human attraction!

At the time, I did not know that Europe had a long tradition of exhibiting people from non-European countries in human zoos, forcing them to dance, drum, or throw spears for the amusement of white audiences. Although these 'ethnological exhibitions' were officially banned in the late 1950s, the colonial gaze clearly lingered in German cultural memory.

No sooner had we left the fenced-in world of the British military base than we found ourselves in what felt like a reenactment of a colonial sideshow. As if we had been placed there for the viewing pleasure of passersby, people whispered about us, pointed fingers, and laughed out loud. Had we charged admission that day, my sisters and I might have made a fortune.

It took me a long time to realize that the white people who stared at me so piercingly that day would later play central roles in my life. That their gazes would follow me everywhere, and eventually, define how I looked at the world and at myself.

In that moment, one thing became crystal clear: there was no going back. I had arrived in Germany. And I was here to stay. So, I reluctantly began to explore my new habitat.

3. Out of Many One People

I am my mother's fourth and last child. Her 'wash belly', as she calls me. In Jamaican communities, the youngest child is often referred to this way. We are said to be lazy and spoiled. I deny ever having been lazy – except on Sundays. As for being spoiled, that is another story: Every time a glass broke or a plate cracked, my older sisters would blame me, believing that as the youngest, I would get into less trouble – which, of course, was not true. In fact, when Mum was angry, you would better stay out of her way, whether you were the reason for her anger or not. The scolding usually came with a cry, carrying the force of a Jamaican woman whose own life story was shaped by struggles, hardship, and adversity.

After a few months in the two-room apartment, my mother announced that she had found a new job, so we moved into a larger apartment where my sisters and I shared rooms two by two. I longed for a room of my own. But my mother told me to be grateful. After all, we lacked nothing, she argued. And she was right: in England, my sisters and I used to top and tail in two beds; in Germany, we shared two rooms. Even my eight-year-old self could recognize this improvement.

But as we all know, money cannot buy everything. Quickly, the downsides of her new job became apparent: unlike other working mothers, mine did not work in an office or a boutique from nine to five. She did not have a lunch break where she could rush home to greet us with a warm meal after school. She worked nights, which I disliked more and more.

In the years that followed, we barely saw her. In the mornings, as I walked to school alone under the watchful eyes of the white villagers, she was asleep. When I came home, she would just be getting up, only to leave the house again shortly afterwards. There were even days when I did not see our mother at all. But when she was home, she was impossible to miss. Her scent filled the room, and her beauty seized me. Yet her job remained a well-kept family secret. In the small conservative village where we lived, we already stood out enough as it was. What would people think if they knew that our mother worked in a night club and that we children were home alone every night?

Adding to this was my father's absence. Out of fear of judgment, my classmates were led to believe that we, too, as a Black family, fit into their conservative norms. So my sisters and I kept quiet about the unusual situation at home. Without yet understanding the patterns that shaped my life, I found myself part of a lineage that stretched back to my extended family in the Caribbean. There, many women raise their children alone. According to the *Jamaican Gleaner*, in 2007 nearly 85 percent of children in Jamaica were born to single mothers. One reason for this is that the marriage rate has declined over the past decade, while the divorce rate has risen. In addition, migration movements, especially since the 1950s, have led many Jamaican men to the USA, Canada, or Great Britain.

Many queer people also leave the island because of the LGBTQIA*-hostile state policies. In Jamaica, homosexuality is a criminal offense, and transphobia part of everyday life. The so-called 'buggery law', which dates back to British colonial times and is still in effect, prescribes forced labour or up to ten years in prison for gay men. According to a 2014 survey, 91 percent of the population support this outdated law and hold hostile views toward homosexual and trans* people. Violent attacks are not uncommon, which is why many queer people flee from the threat of violence. It is usually the mothers who are left behind, solely responsible for raising the children. At the same time, they have to work and take care of the household. The same was true for the women in my family – and later for me. They worked hard, raised the children, and, as a matter of course, managed the household alongside everything else.

When offered the chance to leave the island, it was usually to do care work that eased the burden on white women in North America or Europe and supported their path to emancipation. My grandmother was also given this 'opportunity'. She was part of the Windrush Generation, the name given to Caribbean immigrants who came to Great Britain during and after World War II aboard the *Empire Windrush* to fill the shortage of skilled workers in the care sector. Consequently, there is at least one nurse in almost every Caribbean-British family. In my family, it was my grandmother: Later, one of my sisters also chose this profession.

The most famous Jamaican-British nurse, whom I learned about as early as kindergarten, was Mary Seacole.

Mary Seacole was born in 1805 in Kingston, Jamaica, the daughter of a free Black woman and a white Scottish soldier. Her mother ran a boarding house for sick and wounded soldiers, teaching Mary traditional African and Caribbean healing methods from an early age. In her autobiography, 'Wonderful Adventures of Mrs. Seacole in Many Lands', the first autobiography written by a Black woman in Britain, she described herself as a Creole. After her husband's death, Seacole travelled to England in 1854, hoping to serve as a nurse in the Crimean War. When the British government rejected her offer, she went directly to the front lines and opened a field hospital on her own initiative. Back in London, she worked as the personal masseuse to the Princess of Wales until her death in 1881. In 2016, a statue was erected in her honour on the grounds of St Thomas' Hospital in Lambeth, London.

Since 1962, Jamaica has been politically independent, but economically it continues to struggle with poverty due, in part, to its ongoing membership in the British Commonwealth. And this is unlikely to change any time soon, even after the death of Queen Elizabeth II. She was succeeded as head of state by King Charles III, meaning that the island is still ruled by a white European monarch. Yet, long before this royal transition, the Caribbean nation had been pushing for a break from the British Crown – an understandable demand when we consider how the political relationship has been maintained.

When the so-called Windrush Scandal came to light in 2018, it became clear that the United Kingdom was treating its Black citizens no better than Germany had treated its guest workers. Due to invalidated residency papers, thousands of Black Britons from former colonies lost their jobs and homes, even though they had been living in the country for over 50 years. As a result of Britain's conservative immigration policies, they were suddenly classified as 'illegal immigrants', and many were deported. My grandmother and my aunt were allowed to stay.

My grandmother had immigrated to London in the mid-1960s. She left her children – my mother and my aunt – behind in Jamaica, where they were raised by their grandmother. It was not until my mother was 15 that my grandmother brought her, and later my aunt, to the United Kingdom, making them part of the second generation of Caribbean immigrants. But my mother did not stay there for long. The racist violence, which increasingly escalated and reached its radical peak in the 1981 Brixton riots, was too much to bear. Her marriage to my stepfather and his rank in the military gave her the opportunity to leave the racially charged unrest behind.

After the death of my stepfather, my mother was only allowed to settle in Germany with us children because she had obtained British citizenship at an early stage, which automatically made us children British, as well. Before Brexit, the United Kingdom was part of the European Union, which made it easy for us to obtain a permanent residence permit in Germany. Back then, the residency regulations were not as strict as they are today. But unlike in the United Kingdom, very few people with Jamaican roots live here. And yet, traces of our culture are everywhere: reggae music and dreadlocks have found their way to Germany and taken on a life of their own, even without Black bodies. Today, everyone knows Bob Marley. However, this is where Jamaican history in Germany both begins and ends.

Nevertheless – or perhaps because of this – I began engaging with my Jamaican roots and came to see myself as part of a greater whole early in my life. Before the European colonization of the Caribbean and its foreign designation as the West Indies, there was vibrant inter-Caribbean exchange that extended as far as South America. Individuals from many different cultures and countries came together to form the population. *Out of many one people* is Jamaica's national motto today. Diversity has therefore always been part of our culture, and my sense of community was nurtured from an early age, especially through language, of which my own did not stay the same but evolved and transformed along the way.

The unofficial national language of Jamaica is Patois, a linguistic blend of English and Spanish that my mother would speak whenever she became emotional or angry. As children, we would get a slap on the mouth whenever we tried to imitate the adults. *"Wat'a go an?"* remains a popular greeting on the streets of East London to this day.

And although we were forced to speak the Queen's English, we continued our Afro-cultural traditions in unconventional ways, especially through food: yams, plantains, ackee, and patties – Jamaican specialties that still belong on my shopping list and are often combined with German *Knödel* and gravy today.

Everything I know about the island, however, I had to teach myself: The Indigenous people of Jamaica were called the Taino and belonged to the Arawak people. They, too, contribute to Jamaica's diversity and practiced community. While fleeing European colonial rule, they took in escaped enslaved Africans. Together, they later formed the group known as the Maroons, who, led by the warrior Queen Nanny, resisted the white Europeans.

Queen Nanny was born around 1686 in what is now Ghana. She belonged to the Ashanti people. At the beginning of the 18th century, she and her brothers were captured and enslaved under brutal conditions in Jamaica. Because of the particularly cruel treatment of Black women, the siblings decided to escape shortly after their arrival. Nanny led a group into the mountains, where they founded a village named after her: Nanny Town. She is said to have helped liberate more than 800 enslaved people, leading them not only with strategic skill but also through her knowledge of herbal medicine and her sharing of spiritual practices. Today, Queen Nanny is the only woman listed among Jamaica's National Heroes.

As race is not the central category in Black majority societies, Afro-Caribbean women are more affected by the consequences of the entanglement of imperialist capitalism and sexist patriarchy than by racism. They grow up believing that only education can free them from poverty. There is no other guidance against capitalism, nor any roadmap to feminism. But their success proves them right: many women today are entrepreneurs, doctors, or lawyers, or they take on casual jobs that require fewer qualifications but offer regular pay. As more and more women focus on career and educational goals, birth control plays an important role; family planning has been a consistent focus of Jamaican government policy since the 1950s, as has digitalisation.

In Jamaica, career women are no longer a rarity, and feminism is much more organic than it may appear in Germany and Europe. Actually, Jamaica is also one of the few countries to have been successfully led by a woman: former Prime Minister Portia Simpson-Miller, who served from 2006 to 2007 and again from 2012 to 2016. But feminist success stories from emerging countries remain largely untold. When most Germans think of Jamaica, aside from reggae music, they often envision a tropical paradise populated by eager Black men, catering to the sexual fantasies of white women.

Otherwise, there is the high media presence of exceptional athletic talents. The US-American comedy film *Cool Runnings* achieved worldwide success in the early 1990s. It is based on the true story of a Jamaican bobsled team that participated in the 1988 Winter Olympics in Calgary. Many are also familiar with the Jamaican 'Reggae Boyz', the nickname given to the national men's football team after they qualified for the FIFA World Cup for the first time in 1998.

Female sports stars and legends, however, are far less visible. There is no doubt that Usain Bolt enjoys great popularity in Germany, while female track and field athletes such as Shelly-Ann Fraser-Pryce, who is in no way inferior to him, are likely known to only a few. Some time ago, I also learned about Jamaican professional footballer Beverly Ranger, who even played league football in Germany and gained public attention in 1975 for scoring the 'Goal of the Month'.

In any case, sports – especially track and field – and military service are among the most common ways to escape poverty in Jamaica. And many aspire to follow these routes, as there is a bitter struggle against classism, not racism. Instead of racist police violence, there is class-based police violence. According to Amnesty International, the rate of fatal police shootings is one of the highest in the world. The most frequent victims are poor Black men who are accused of criminal activity. In addition, poor women, queer people, and orphaned children are also imprisoned, tortured, and murdered. With these brutal measures, the government tries to contain poverty without actually addressing its structural causes. I can say with certainty that, like my sense of community, anti-capitalism was instilled in me from birth.

Through the legacy of Afro-Caribbean visiting professor Audre Lorde, who visited Berlin repeatedly in the 1980s and 90s, I would later learn to reconcile my lived differences with my inner rather than my external world, and fight against racism, sexism, and capitalism.

But it took a long journey before I reached this point and could openly say that I am a radical Black feminist – and proudly German.

Anhad Arora
The Worlds of German Song Programme Notes for the Recital

The soundscapes of the German Lied may be mistaken for being parochial. The invocation of forests, mountains, Wirtshäuser, the Augsburger Dom, in some of the best-known works continually re-anchors the Lied in local rather than 'exotic' geographies. The recital programme performed at the Association for German Studies conference in Oxford in 2025 was designed to challenge this conception by programming the works of nineteenth-century composers who occupy peripheral positions on the recital platform. Through Orientalism and translations of European folksong, poets and composers used the intimate means of the Lied to imagine both seductive and dangerous worlds. The purpose of the notes below is to provide a brief background to the individual items in the programme.[20]

Title page of Johann Wolfgang von Goethe, *West-östlicher Divan* (Case 2.1) Taylorian ARCH.8°.G.1819

---

[20] The material is partly based on my doctoral dissertation '*Divan* Dialogues: Orientalism and the Lied, 1814–1840', which will soon be available on ORA.

Setting of 'Suleika' by Fenny Hensel, illustrated by Wilhelm Hensel
Part of an autograph album for Cécile Mendelssohn Bartholdy
Bodleian Libraries, University of Oxford. MS. M. Deneke Mendelssohn b. 2, fol. 10r

1. Carl Friedrich Zelter, 'Suleika'

Unpublished, 1820.

S u l e i k a.

Ach! um deine feuchten Schwingen,
West, wie sehr ich dich beneide:
Denn du kannst ihm Kunde bringen
Was ich in der Trennung leide.

Die Bewegung deiner Flügel
Weckt im Busen stilles Sehnen,
Blumen, Augen, Wald und Hügel
Stehn bey deinem Hauch in Thränen.

Doch dein mildes sanftes Wehen
Kühlt die wunden Augenlieder;
Ach für Leid müfst' ich vergehen,
Hofft' ich nicht zu sehn ihn wieder.

Eile denn zu meinem Lieben,
Spreche sanft zu seinem Herzen;
Doch vermeid' ihn zu betrüben
Und verbirg ihm meine Schmerzen.

Sag ihm, aber sag's bescheiden:
Seine Liebe sey mein Leben,
Freudiges Gefühl von beyden
Wird mir seine Nähe geben.

> *Ah, West-wind, for thy dewy wing*
>   *How sorely must I envy thee!*
> *For tidings thou to him canst bring*
>   *Of grief his absence lays on me.*
>
> *The wavings of thy pinions light*
>   *Wake silent yearning in the heart;*
> *From flowers and eyes, from wood and height,*
>   *Breathed on by thee, the quick tears start.*
>
> *Yet these soft wanderings of thy breath*
>   *Cool my hurt eyelids and restore;*
> *Ah, I should faint with pain to death*
>   *Hoped I not sight of him once more.*
>
> *Haste then to my belovèd, haste,*
>   *Speak to his heart in gentlest strain;*
> *No shade across his spirit cast,*
>   *And hide, ah, hide from him my pain!*
>
> *Tell him, but tell with lips discreet,*
>   *His love's the life by which I live!*
> *Glad sense where life with love shall meet*
>   *His nearness to my heart will give.*[21]

From the late 1790s to their deaths in 1832, Zelter and Goethe were close friends. The two maintained a lengthy correspondence in which everything, and not simply music, was discussed both seriously and playfully – from 1812 in the 'Du' form. Zelter famously would take on the function of Goethe's musical partner and consultant, the latter sending over 'singable' poems to set once they had been completed. One of their collaborations revolved around the *West-östlicher Divan* from which Zelter's 'Suleika' comes. Zelter was privy

---

[21] The text is based on Johann Wolfgang von Goethe, *West-östlicher Divan*, 'Buch Suleika', Stuttgart 1819, p. 166–167, see facsimile on preceding page. The poem is one of those written by Marianne von Willemer. The translation is by Dowden (1914, see catalogue 2.1., also for the illustration on p. 32).

to the collection's gestation, beginning in summer of 1814, with the composer producing part-song renditions of Goethe's responses to the Persian poet, Hafis (c. 1325–1390). Many of Zelter's early poems and settings, which were transmitted by manuscripts and handed over in person, entered the repertory of the *Liedertafel*, a male-voice singing institution founded in 1808–1809.

The eventual publication of the *Divan* in 1819, which comprised twelve 'books' of poetry, including the *Buch Suleika*, and a set of socio-cultural notes designed to give the uninitiated reader an insight into Goethe's novel Orientalist world, was met with a degree of reserve from both the literary and musical public. The hybrid novelties that in our time mark the text out as an exceptional piece of European Orientalism – from the title, through the ornamented cartouche on the title page, the Persian ossia titles, the poetry, to the *Noten und Abhandlungen* – did as much to repel as attract contemporary musicians on the search for fresh texts.

Despite being one of the collection's intimates, even Zelter battled with translating Goethe's Orientalism into a musically communicable form. He produced only a handful of solo settings of the *Divan* following the collection's publication. Three of these, including his setting of 'Ach um deine feuchten Schwingen' were left unpublished during his lifetime. 'Suleika' is composed strophically, following Zelter's and Goethe's singable ideal, with one melody and accompaniment designed to fit the general sentiment of each varying stanza of verse.

2. Carl Loewe, 'Beim Tanze' and 'Des Jünglings Segen'

From *Sechs Serbenlieder, op.* 15 (publ. 1825).

Beim Tanze

Trallallala! Mein Liebchen!
Was hast mir nicht gesagt,
Daß krank mein Liebster worden,
Hätt' gerne leckerbißchen
Ihm zur Nahrung geboten:
Vom Mückchen, das Rippenstückchen,
Vom Fliegelein, das Seelchen klein,
Vom Krebse zwei Bein',
Ein Becherlein mit Branntewein,
Ihm zum Geschenke,
Daß satt sich tränke,
Der Liebste mein!

At the dance

Trallallala! My darling! Why did you not tell me that my beloved had fallen ill? I would gladly have offered him delicacies to nourish and comfort him: from the gnat, a morsel of rib; from the little fly, its tiny soul; from the crab, two legs; and a small cup of brandy as a gift, that he, my dearest love, might drink his fill! (Translation Henrike Lähnemann)

Des Jünglings Segen

Singt ein Falk' all' die Nacht durch,
Dicht vor den Fenstern des Milan:
"Auf, und erwache, o Milan!
Es vermählt sich Dein Mädchen,
Ladet Dich ein zu der Hochzeit;
Oder willst Du nicht kommen:
Sollst Deinen Segen ihr senden!"

"Laß Sie sich vermählen, laß sie!
Kommen nicht mag ich zur Hochzeit,
Aber ich send; ihr den Segen:
Nimmer einen Knaben gebär' sie!
So viel Brot sie verzehret,
So viel Weh erdulde sie!
So viel Wasser sie trinket,
So viel Thränen vergieße sie!" –

The Young Man's Blessing

A falcon sings all through the night, just outside the windows of the kite: "Awake, milan, arise! Your girl is to be married; she invites you to the wedding. And if you will not come, you must send her your blessing!"

"Let her marry, let her! I cannot attend the wedding, but I shall send her my blessing: may she never bear a son! As much bread as she consumes, so much sorrow may she endure; as much water as she drinks, so many tears may she shed!" (Translation Henrike Lähnemann)

Carl Loewe (1796–1869) wore many hats. He held the position of Music Director in Stettin (now Szczecin in Poland), and taught music, the sciences, Greek, and *Universalgeschichte* at the local gymnasium. These wide-reaching interests shaped his print persona. Beyond songs, his bibliography included a treatise on the pedagogical use of singing in schools, and the first philological commentary of Goethe's *Faust II*, published in 1834. Although Loewe's balladry calls forth the uncanny spectres of the Romantic, the composer's broader intellectual outlook could be described as enlightened.

Loewe's intellectual pursuits informed his compositional practice. The composer took an interest in representing the gamut of literature translated into German. The *Gesamtausgabe* of his songs compiled at the turn of the twentieth century features German-language songs on French, Nordic, Scottish, Spanish, Polish, and Orientalist themes and figures. These songs were grouped, at times misleadingly, by his editor Max Runze into 'national' classes, capitalising on

Loewe's reputation as a composer with a painterly eye for local detail and 'objectivity'. Contemporary audiences, however, would have heard Loewe's songs with precisely this expectation. Loewe was known to self-accompany his songs on wide-ranging concert tours: a modern, itinerant German bard singing translated Serbian folksongs.

Strangely, the *Serbenlieder* are not given their own 'national' category in Runze's scheme, but they were published as a self-standing volume in 1826. Loewe's musical language is studiedly *volkstümlich*. Loewe eschews the trappings of the longer, sectional form of the ballad for which he was renowned in favour of small, simple accompaniments and 'singable' melodies. There is perhaps a hint of 'local colour' in the use of pedal points and the modal-minor mixture, though whether these were culled from Serbian melodies or worked as signifiers of folksiness is moot.

The poems were collected by Vuk Stefanović Karadžić (1787–1864) and translated by Loewe's sister-in-law, Therese Amalie Luise von Jacob (1797–1870).[22] The first letters of her name made up her pseudonym, 'Talvj'. Talvj mentions in the preface to the *Volkslieder der Serben* that Karadžić's collection came to the attention of the literary community in 1814–1815, with the publication of two volumes in Vienna. A decade later, in 1824, the Serbian poet was known enough for Jacob Grimm to publish a translation of his *Kleine serbische Grammatik* in Berlin. Though Herder springs to mind as Talvj's model, it appears to have been Goethe who provided an impulse for her engagement with the 'foreign' in the *Volkslieder,* the first edition containing a poetic 'Zueignung' to Goethe.

---

[22] The songs are close translations of traditional Serbian songs from the first volume of *Srpske narodne pjesme*. The original titles are *Dragom ponude* (*Offerings to the dear one*), to which Vuk S. Karadžić adds *kad se igra* (*when dancing*), 263rd in part XIV which collects songs to be sung while dancing (*što se pjevaju u kolu*), and *Blagosov* (a northern Serbian dialectal form of the word *blagoslov, blessing*), number 362 in part XIX which contains love songs. With thanks to Omer Mihović for the information.

An Göthe.

Volkslieder der Serben. Metrisch übersetzt und historisch eingeleitet von Talvj Haller & Leipzig 1835, 2nd ed., Taylorian 59.C.25 T.1, vol. 1, p. V.

In Nacht versenkt, in meiner Jugend Tagen,
Reißt mich ein Ton aus fernem Ost empor;
Und wie die Lüft' ihn nah und näher tragen,
Lockt er die Seel' aus kranker Brust hervor.
Und sie vernimmt die wundersamsten Sagen,
Lauscht willenlos, doch bald mit durst'gem Ohr,
Und fühlt, wie am lebendig-frischen Sinne
Auch sie erstark und neue Kraft gewinne.

Und leih' ich mich als Botin diesen Tönen,
Worin der Geist der Fremde sich erschloß,
Nicht mühvoll darffst Du dich dem Klang gewöhnen,
Der seltsam oft dem Sängermund entfloß. [...]

Immersed in night, in the days of my youth, I am suddenly lifted by a tone from the distant East. As the breeze carries it ever closer, it draws forth the soul from a weary breast. The soul begins to hear the most wondrous tales, at first passively, but soon with eager ears, and feels how, through the vivid freshness of the senses, it too gains strength and renewed vitality.

And if I lend myself as a messenger to these tones, in which the spirit of the foreign world is revealed, you need not labour to accustom yourself to the sound, which often escapes the singer's lips in strange fashion.
(Translation Henrike Lähnemann)

3. Theodor Fröhlich, 'Du meine Seele'

No. 4 from *Persische Lieder, op. 12* (publ. 1834).

Du meine Seele, du mein Herz,
Du meine Wonn', o du mein Schmerz,
Du meine Welt, in der ich lebe,
Mein Himmel du, darein ich schwebe,
O du mein Grab, in das hinab
Ich ewig meinen Kummer gab!
Du bist die Ruh, du bist der Frieden,
Du bist vom Himmel mir beschieden.
Dass du mich liebst, macht mich mir wert,
Dein Blick hat mich vor mir verklärt,
Du hebst mich liebend über mich,
Mein guter Geist, mein bess'res Ich!

You, my soul, you, my heart, you, my delight, oh you, my pain, you, my world, in which I live; my heaven, into which I float; oh you, my grave, into which I have forever laid my sorrow. You are the rest, you are the peace, you are destined by heaven for me. That you love me gives me worth in my own eyes; your gaze has transfigured me before myself. You raise me lovingly above myself, my guiding spirit, my better self.
(Translation Henrike Lähnemann)

The Swiss composer Theodor Fröhlich (1803–1836) is perhaps the obscurest of the composers featured in the programme. He studied in Berlin in 1826, as many did, with Zelter, who was also chiefly responsible for the Mendelssohns' musical education, and with Bernhard Klein (1793–1832), himself an erstwhile student of Zelter's, before returning to the canton of Aargau, where he took on provincial musical duties in the early 1830s. His end was as tragic as it was Romantic: by suicide.

All of Fröhlich's texts in the op. 14 come from Friedrich Rückert (1788–1866). Much like Schubert's 'Erlkönig', which in fame and status has overshadowed all other essays, Rückert's 'Du meine Seele, du mein Herz' is principally known through Schumann's setting, 'Widmung', published as the opening number of his *Myrthen, op. 25* and given to Clara Wieck as a wedding gift in September 1840. Schumann's 'dedicatory' title was his own paratextual addition. Rückert has no title.

That Fröhlich decided to include the title 'Persische Lieder' shows how keenly composers were aware of the interpretative work that could be read across from the biographies of their poets. For as well as being one of the moderns of German poetry, Rückert was one of the leading Orientalists of his day. He held professorships in Erlangen and Berlin, could read over forty languages, and composed both academic and non-specialist Orientalist *Nachdichtungen* and translations, among them a posthumously published rhyming rendering of the Qur'an.

An important influence on the Rückert's Orientalist development was Goethe. Like Talvj, Rückert began his *Oestliche Rosen* (publ. 1822) with a dedicatory poem to Goethe. Rückert specifically noted his indebtedness to the *Divan*, which composers and readers alike must have recognised:

> Zu Goethe's west-östlichem Diwan
>
> Wollt ihr kosten
> Reinen Osten
> Müßt ihr gehn von hier zum selben Manne,
> Der vom Westen
> Auch den besten
> Wein von jeher schenkt' aus voller Kanne.
> Als der West war durchgekostet,
> Hat er nun den Ost entmostet; [...]

On Goethe's 'West-Eastern Divan'

If you wish to savour the pure East, you must go from here to the very same man who also from the West has always poured the finest wine from a brimming jug. Once he had thoroughly tasted the West, he then proceeded to press the essence from the East.

𝔒𝔢𝔰𝔱𝔩𝔦𝔠𝔥𝔢 𝔑𝔬𝔰𝔢𝔫

von

𝔉𝔯𝔦𝔢𝔡𝔯𝔦𝔠𝔥 𝔑ü𝔠𝔨𝔢𝔯𝔱.

𝔇𝔯𝔢𝔦 𝔏𝔢𝔰𝔢𝔫.

Friedrich Rückert, Östliche Rosen. Drei Lesen, Leipzig: Brockhaus 1822 Bodleian Library, 8° gamma 37 BS, title page

Fröhlich's designation 'Persische Lieder' thus at once provides insight into Fröhlich's own conception of Rückert's poetry and a hint to his musical audience. The performing public was also to understand these songs as 'Persian songs'. The doubleness of the text, the repeated mentions of the 'Du', becomes a form of engagement and address with an imagined, paradisal Orientalist world, which we can now read across to Schumann's vaunted setting.

4. Fanny Hensel, 'Hausgarten'

Unpublished, 1840.

Hier sind wir nun vorerst ganz still zu Haus,
Von Tür zu Türe sieht es lieblich aus,
Der Künstler froh die stillen Blicke hegt,
Wo Leben sich zum Leben freundlich regt.

Und wie wir auch durch fremde Lande ziehn,
Dort kommt es her, dort kehrt es wieder hin,
Wir wenden uns, wie auch die Welt entzücke,
Der Enge zu, die uns allein, allein beglücke.

Here we are, for the time being, quietly at home. From door to door, the view is charming. The artist joyfully cherishes these tranquil glances, where life stirs life in friendly motion.

And even as we travel through foreign lands, it is from here that it originates, and to here that it returns. However enchanting the world may be, we turn towards the narrowness that alone, and only it, brings us true happiness. (Translation Henrike Lähnemann)

This setting of 'Hausgarten' by Fanny Hensel (1805–1847) closes the 'Reise-Album', which was put together with her husband, Wilhelm Hensel (1794–1861), to commemorate their travels to Italy in 1839–1840. Fanny had to this point relatively few opportunities to travel by comparison with her brother, Felix. One early family trip to Switzerland in 1822 left a lasting impression, not least because the family stopped off in Weimar on their way back, where Fanny would play both her compositions and examples of Bach to Goethe's delight.

The debate surrounding the various impediments to Fanny publishing songs, which include conservative familial views of class and gender held by both her brother and father, still rages. But the contemporary public's loss is our archival gain. Both the Hensels, husband and wife, collaborated on songs designed for private and semi-public viewing, with Wilhelm, the court painter, often decorating her works with vignettes (see Case 2.1). Their work is now preserved in the Bodleian Library in Oxford and the Staatsbibliothek zu Berlin.

The 'Reise-Album' provides one such example. It opens with a beautiful frontispiece, which depicts 'Deutschland' giving 'Italien' the Hensels' album of songs, a true *Liedergabe*. 'Hausgarten' also features a drawing, which represents steps leading up to a foliaged entrance. We now know that this is a depiction of the Hensels' own home, the *Gartenhaus* of the family compound on Leipziger Straße in Berlin. The choice is all the more moving, since Goethe's poem tells of returning to the comforts of the home after travel 'durch fremde Lande'. Together with the opening number in the collection, 'Nach Süden', this song provides a fitting frame for the musical-visual musings of their own Italian journey.

Italian literature with the torch, furthest left of the four statues of the Taylorian
Photograph Henrike Lähnemann

5. Niels Gade, 'Meinen Kranz hab' ich gesendet' & 'Wenn der letzte Saum des Tages'

Ns. 2 and 5, from *Bilder des Orients, op. 24* (publ. c. 1852).

> Meinen Kranz hab' ich gesendet,
> Aber nicht, dich zu beglücken;
> Schweigend sollt' er dir verkünden
> Meiner Seele bangen Schmerz.
>
> Unsre Rosse stehn gesattelt,
> Fort nach Schiras eilt der Vater;
> Horch, er ruft! – Von der Geliebten
> Nimm ein zitternd Lebewohl.

I have sent my garland, but not to bring you joy; silently it was meant to convey the anxious pain of my soul.
Our horses are saddled, and my father hastens away to Shiraz. Listen—he calls! Take a trembling farewell from the woman you love.
(Translation Henrike Lähnemann)

> Wenn der letzte Saum des Tages
> In dem Arm der Nacht gesunken
> Und der Ruf der zehnten Stunde
> Von dem Minaret erschallt;
> Dann im Laubengang der Myrthen,
> Wo die rothen Rosen duften,
> Darfst du meine Küsse fragen,
> Ob dir Fatme nahe sey.

When the final edge of day has sunk into the arms of night, and the call of the tenth hour echoes from the minaret, then, in the myrtle-covered walkway where the red roses exude their fragrance, you may ask my kisses whether Fatme is near you. (Translation Henrike Lähnemann)

The Danish composer Niels Gade (1817–1890), Robert Schumann wrote, was 'nourished by the poetry of his fatherland: he knows and loves its poets; old legends and traditions [...]'. His prominence in mid-century musical life was further evidence of the gradual 'emancipation' of the 'nations bordering Germany' from 'the influence of German music'. Here, however, Gade eschews the putative 'Northern musical character' of the 'Ossian' overture or Danish folksong. His op. 24 brings together the familiar alliance of the German Lied and German Orientalism.

The texts Gade selected came from Heinrich Stieglitz's *Bilder des Orients* (publ. four volumes, 1831–1833). Although little known in our time, Stieglitz (1801–1849) was a prominent musical personality in Berlin in the 1820s and early 1830s. He wrote paeans to Beethoven and Weber, both of which were performed onstage in Leipzig, the former subsequently published in the *Berliner allgemeine musikalische Zeitung*; and worked enterprisingly as the editor of the *Berliner Musen-Almanach* in 1830, for whom he managed to secure the first publication of Goethe's late-Orientalist cycle, the *Chinesisch-deutsche Jahres- und Tageszeiten*.

The 'Stieglitz' that scholarship has remembered is Charlotte (1806–1834), the poet's wife, who committed suicide in 1834. The act caused a scandal. She took the dagger Heinrich had given her and stabbed herself. Her reason was to inspire Heinrich to great poetic achievements. Young Germans, Theodor Mundt in particular, saw in her death a symbol and warning for 1830s literary culture. Heinrich, meanwhile, could not fulfil his wife's literary hopes. His years following her death were marked by wandering and reflection. He eventually died in Venice in 1849. Gade would have certainly known of the tragedy. Lexicon entries from 1834 routinely mention Charlotte and Heinrich in one breath. In the Taylorian copy (Case 2.1.), Heinrich Stieglitz is identified on the title-page as 'husband of Charlotte, née Willhöfft'.

Thanks to the advocacy of his friends and networks, Stieglitz's Orientalist *Bilder* inspired a wave of songs in the first half of the 1830s.

Stieglitz modelled himself after Goethe, and believed that music was a natural complement to, even a completion of, a 'singable' poem. Like Goethe, he would send his texts to his own musical partner, the influential critic, composer, and theoretician, Adolph Bernhard Marx, who advocated for the collection in print. The *Bilder*'s fizz had simmered down significantly by the late 1840s. In that sense, Gade's op. 24 was somewhat belated.

> **3.**
> **Fatme.**
> (Vom Balcone.)
>
> Wenn der letzte Saum des Tages
> In den Arm der Nacht gesunken
> Und der Ruf der zehnten Stunde
> Von dem Minaret erschallt;
> Dann im Laubengang der Myrthen,
> Wo die rothen Rosen duften,
> Darfst du meine Küsse fragen,
> Ob dir Fatme nahe sey.

Heinrich Stieglitz, Bilder des Orients, vol 2, no. 3 'Fatme, p. 141 (Case 2.1.)
Taylorian, FIEDLER.K.4050.1/2

Both 'Meinen Kranz hab' ich gesendet' and 'Wenn der letzte Saum des Tages' are taken from the poetic cycle 'Ali und Fatme' from volume 2 on 'Persien', and thematise *Blumensprache*, the riddling language of flowers, which had been long associated with 'Oriental' assignations. Goethe's *Noten und Abhandlungen*, which Stieglitz read assiduously, contained an essay on 'Blumen- und Zeichenwechsel', even providing a list of rhyming pairs: 'Amarante – Ich sah und brannte'; 'Jasmin – Nimm mich hin'. This was to be understood as eroticism, sublimation, and innuendo. The topic allowed composers to hint at, if not graphically represent, forbidden pleasure, a trope long associated with the Orient.

6. Heinrich Marschner, 'An Suleika'

From *Lieder, op. 115* (publ.1843). Translation HL.

O, wär' ich vom Berge der junge Aar,
Und schwäng' gleich dem Wetter mein Flügelpaar,
Dann würd ich, Suleika, schnell tragen dich fort,
Hinauf in mein Wohnhaus, auf's Felsenmeer dort!
Deine Speise wären Wolken, und Strahlen dein Trank!

O, wär' ich ein Kampfroß, das stolz und leicht
Durch Fluren und Auen wie Sturmwind fleucht,
Dann würd' ich, Suleika, dich bringen in's Thal,
Wo freier das Blachfeld durchströmt der Ural!
Deine Speise wären Blumen, und Düfte dein Trank!

O, wär' ich ein Raubthier im dunklen Wald,
Und wären die Höhlen mein Aufenthalt,
Dann würd' ich, Suleika, dich rauben, fürwahr,
Hinab in die Klüfte, trotz Kampfroß und Aar!
Deine Speise wäre Waldsang, und Kühle dein Trank!

Oh, if only I were a young eagle from the mountain, and my wings swept through the air like a storm, then I would swiftly carry you away, Suleika, to my dwelling high above, on the sea of rocks! Your food would be the clouds, and your drink the rays of light.

Oh, if only I were a warhorse, proud and nimble, galloping through fields and meadows like a tempest, then I would bring you, Suleika, to the valley where the open plain is freely traversed by the Ural! Your food would be flowers, and your drink the fragrances of the air.

Oh, if only I were a wild beast in the dark forest, and the caves were my home, then I would steal you away, Suleika, indeed I would, down into the chasms, defying both warhorse and eagle! Your food would be the songs of the woods, and your drink the coolness of the shade.
(Translation Henrike Lähnemann)

The *Divan* 'Suleika' who sings in Zelter's song has a Persian literary provenance. Goethe's took Suleika from the Persian poet, Jami, who tells the story of Potiphar's wife transfixed by the beauty of Yusuf. Goethe keeps Suleika but replaces an older man, Hatem, for the much younger Yusuf. Suleika and Hatem were literary analogues for Marianne von Willemer and Goethe, the former authoring some of the *Divan*'s poems, including 'Was bedeutet die Bewegung' and 'Ach, um deine feuchten Schwingen'.

Heinrich Marschner's 'An Suleika' is thus a false friend. In the original publication, Marschner (1795–1861) clearly subtitles the song 'Baschkirenlied von K. Ch. Tenner', perhaps to draw the public's attention to the fact that this is a different Suleika who is being addressed. While it is difficult to identify Marschner's textual source, Tenner's 'Baschkirenlied', which purported to be translated 'nach dem Russischen', was published in the *Morgenblatt für gebildete Leser* in January 1842. Marschner's collection appeared the following year.

The song itself presents the menacing threat of abduction, set somewhere in Urals. Marschner's music is suitably dramatic. The accompaniment comprises moto perpetuo triplets in C minor, which reminds of Schubert's 'Erstarrung' from *Winterreise*, while the voice sings three verses to the same melody, each ending with a varied poetic refrain.

Stieglitz, Lieder für Tenor oder Sopran und Piano, p. 12.

German in the World
Exhibition Catalogue

Figure representing German Literature above the portico of the Taylorian
Photograph Henrike Lähnemann

Case 1: German in the World. Introduction

Models of melancholia: Walther von der Vogelweide, Dürer's *Melencolia I*, and the statue representing German literature in display case 1 of the exhibition
Photograph Henrike Lähnemann

> [...] *ich hete in mîne hant gesmogen*
> *daz kinne und ein mîn wange.*
> *dô dâhte ich mir vil ange,*
> *wie man zer welte solte leben.*
> ([...] I had put the chin and one of my cheeks into my hand; there I was anxiously thinking what might be the right way to live in this world. HL)

These lines, by Walther von der Vogelweide, part of his best-known Sangspruch reflective on the state of the world, show that linking German and the world has a long tradition. The group of sculptures above the entrance to the Taylor Institution Library, putting the figure of German literature among three other world languages: French, Italian, and Spanish, also embodies this frame of mind.

In honour of the meeting of the Association of German Studies, this exhibition aims to put the topic 'German in the World' in a historic and literary context, as reflected in the holdings of the Taylor Institution Library, the oldest and largest Modern Languages library in the country.

The exhibition presents case studies from the canonical to the contemporary, foregrounding the role of books and librarians as cultural ambassadors. Each display case reflects one aspect of the overall topic; it has been curated by a mixed group of Germanists: librarian Emma Huber, lecturer Henrike Lähnemann, alumna Christina Ostermann, doctoral student Santhia Velasco Kittlaus, and Siegbert Prawer Prize winner Anhad Arora.

1.1. Thinking German Literature

The thinking woman statue with her head in hand, representing German, draws on a long tradition of picturing philosophers and thinkers as melancholic people. Famous German predecessors are the depiction of Walther von der Vogelweide in the two illuminated collections of Minnesang, the Weingartner Liederhandschrift and the Codex Manesse, and *Melencolia I*, one of the so-called Meisterstiche by Albrecht Dürer.

Die Minnesinger in Bildern der Manessischen Handschrift, Insel-Bücherei Nr. 450, ed. by Hans Naumann (Leipzig: Im Insel-Verlag 1933) Taylorian ZA.556.GER

The Insel-Bücherei, with its distinctive art deco paper covers and title labels, was one of the most successful popularisers of German literature and art, providing affordable collectibles for bibliophiles without a large budget. The volume of 24 reproductions of author images from the iconic *Codex Manesse* was re-issued 15 times with the final edition in 1965.

Erwin Panofsky / Fritz Saxl, *Dürers 'Melencolia I', eine quellen- und typengeschichtliche Untersuchung*, Leipzig 1923 (Studien der Bibliothek Warburg 2), Taylorian Soc. 3975 d.93 (no.2(1923))

Panofsky and Saxl trace the ancestry of Dürer's engraving back to Aristotelean philosophy, texts about Saturnus by Abû Ma'šar and Ibn Esra, images developed by Henry of Gent and the *Libri de vita triplic* by Marsilio Ficino in the Florentine Renaissance, showing the global circulation of ideas. This was a foundational text for the study of iconography established by Aby Warburg, published before his library had to emigrate from Hamburg to London in 1933.

Photograph of the Taylor Institution before the extension of 1932. c1880s, Oxford, Bodleian Libraries, University Archives, TL 5/11

The four statues by William Grinsell Nicholl (1796-1871) represent the four modern languages taught in Oxford in the 19th century. The plinths are engraved with the names of philosophers and authors, Dante, Guicciardini and Tasso representing Italy; Racine, Molière and Montesquieu France; Goethe, Herder and Schiller Germany; and Calderón, Cervantes and Mariana Spain.

1.2. Historic Acquisitions of German Material

Making German literature from all periods accessible in its original form, in translation, and commentary, has been at the heart of Germanistik in Oxford, and has also shaped the acquisition policy of the Taylorian; thus the extensive run of original Reformation pamphlets resulted from Max Müller's attempt to counter what he saw as Oxford's lack of theological rigour. At the same time, donations added collections that are unexpected, quirky, and characteristic of their times. Items such as the lock of Goethe's hair speaks of the Geniekult of the 19th century. The Taylorian had become known as the home for German literature, even in the form of non-literary memorabilia.

A Medieval Miscellany from Erfurt, Taylor Institution: MS 8° G. 1;
  Daniela Raidel, *Beschreibung der Handschrift Oxford, Taylor Institution, MS 8° G. 1* (1999), Taylor Institution: MS 8° G. 1/1.
The manuscript has figured in History of the Book projects in courses taught by Nigel Palmer and Henrike Lähnemann and was included in the catalogue by Bálazs Nemes of the Erfurt Charterhaus.

Deuttung der grewlichen figur des Munchkalbs tzu Freyburg in Meyssen gfunden
  (Erfurt 1523) ARCH.8°.G.1523(8) and the Taylor Edition Monk calf (vol. 6), ed. Florian Gieseler, Henrike Lähnemann, Tim Powell, Oxford: Taylor Editions 2023. Hans Sachs: Canon and Cobbler (1524) as original and as edition in the Treasures of the Taylorian (Taylor Institution: ARCH.8°.G.1524(26) and private loan)
Two Reformation pamphlets acquired via the special funds administered by Friedrich Max Müller through the librarian Heinrich Krebs from Heidelberg duplicates.

Lock of Goethe's hair, framed, with a pressed viol (?) and two notes
  Taylorian MS. 8° G. 26
The lock came as a donation to the Taylorian, showing how memorabilia were part of the export industry of Weimar Classicism. With the lock are the two envelopes in which it was enclosed, as authentication of the 'relic' which a barber cut from Goethe's hair after it had grown long during an illness.

56 *Catalogue*

Case 1.2: Goethe's Hair with authentication notes in English and German
Photograph Henrike Lähnemann

1) *Goethe's Haar: Diese Locke(n) wurden ihm am 2ten März 1823 in den Tagen seiner Genesung von der Krankheit abgeschnitten.*

2) *Goethe's Hair: Given me by my Aunt, Mrs Gabriele Saeltzer, of Weimar, the only surviving child of my Father's Uncle, Johannes Daniel Falk, the Satirist & Friend of Goethe. Given me at Cotsclough, Cheshire on Fri., Aug. 19. 1881 H John Falk*

1.3. Current Engagement with the Oxford Holdings

Working with bi- or multilingual authors who cross the boundaries of national literature has been one of the focus points for inviting Writers in Residence and for sponsoring students to engage with translation and creative adaptation of German literature.

Twin Spin: 17 Shakespeare Sonnets, ed. by Draesner, Cheesman, Lähnemann, and Huber (2016), Exhibition Catalogue 'Shall I Compare Thee? Shakespeare in Translation'.
Yoko Tawada in Dialogue, ed. by Held, Lähnemann, and Lloyd (2018), Exhibition Catalogue 'Von der Muttersprache zur Sprachmutter'.
Tara Williams, *Bamberg: an Anthology* (2025).
Hedwig Dohm, *The Woman You Become: Werde, die du bist!* (2025), ed. by Martine, transl. by Dicker, Mckinley-Smith, Neill, and Reese.
German in the World Exhibition catalogue, ed. by Lähnemann, Ostermann (2025).

This volume is the latest in a series of volumes of 'Writers in Residence' and 'Cultural Memory', open access available.

Kafka – Making of an Icon, ed. by Ritchie Robertson, with contributions by Carolin Duttlinger, Barry Murnane, Katrin Kohl, Meindert Peters, and Karolina Watroba (Bodleian Exhibition Catalogue 2024, link)
Facsimile of one of Kafka's Hebrew vocab booklets, Bodleian Library, MS. Kafka 33, part of the Kafka papers at the Bodleian Library (private loan, blog post)
Franz Kafka, *The metamorphosis and other stories*, Oxford: OUP 2024, Taylorian 838.1/K11.

One of the most important German literary assets of Oxford are the Kafka papers which are shared with the Literaturarchiv Marbach. For the 100th anniversary of Kafka's death, the Bodleian Library staged a large exhibition about the global reach of Kafka – and the Taylorian had a small, student-curated exhibition on Kafka's Languages. Additionally, Kafka's Metamorphoses became the first book read collectively by all of Oxford, in a special edition 'Oxford reads Kafka' designed for the anniversary.

Case 2: *West-Eastern Divan* & *Ringparabel*

Case 2.1: At the back the 'New Divan' with the motif of the Gingko Biloba leaf
Photograph Henrike Lähnemann

2.1. Goethe's Divan at the centre of a tradition

> Nord und West und Süd zersplittern,
> Throne bersten, Reiche zittern:
> Flüchte du, im reinen Osten
> Patriarchenluft zu kosten!
> Unter Lieben, Trinken, Singen
> Soll dich Chisers Quell verjüngen.
>
> Johann Wolfgang von Goethe,
> *West-östlicher Divan*, opening poem 'Hegire'

Hammer-Purgstall, Joseph, Freiherr von: *Der Diwan von Mohammed Schemsed-din Hafis. Aus dem Persischen zum erstenmal ganz übersetzt...*, (Tübingen: Cotta'sche Buchhandlung 1812/13) 2 vols, Bodleian Ary. 3.420a/b

This collection of translations of the Persian poet Hafis by the Viennese Orientalist Joseph von Hammer was as trailblazing as it was influential. As the translator describes in the preface to the edition, Hafis' research, though international and cosmopolitan, was woefully incomplete in the first decade of the nineteenth century. Hammer reports that only 'a seventh' of his work had been translated. Goethe's publisher, Cotta, first sent him a copy of Hammer's work May 1814, which inspired Goethe to his own *Divan*. The famous *Chiffrenbriefe* between Goethe and Marianne von Willemer used Hammer's volume as the basis for a poetic conversation. More broadly, Hammer's endeavours, including the *Geschichte der schönen Redekünste Persiens* (1818) and his edited *Fundgruben des Orients* (1809–1818) were essential reading for budding Orientalists.

Heinrich Stieglitz, *Bilder des Orients* in 4 vols., (Leipzig: E. Enobloch 1831). (Taylorian, FIEDLER.K.4050.1/2) available via Google Books.
Johann Wolfgang von Goethe, *West-östlicher Divan* (Stuttgart: Cotta'sche Buchhandlung 1819), Taylorian ARCH.8°.G.1819, Google Books
The first edition of Goethe's *West-östlicher Divan* is both peculiar and beautiful. It contains a specially designed ornamented cartouche and Goethe's socio-cultural essays, 'Besserem Verständniss', which were in later collected-works editions split up from the poetry proper and

published in a separate volume under the forbidding title, *Noten und Abhandlungen zu besserem Verständniss des west-östlichen Divans*. In the first edition, however, the essays seamlessly flow on from the twelve books of poetry, with a quatrain serving as a transition.

> *Besserem Verständnifs.*
>
> Wer das Dichten will verstehen
> Mufs in's Land der Dichtung gehen;
> Wer den Dichter will verstehen
> Mufs in Dichters Lande gehen.

Motto page (quire 16, p. 1) of the commentary part of the *Divan* Taylor Institution Library, ARCH.8°.G.1819

In its first printed form, the *Divan* is thus a two-part work, containing both poetry and prose. This, together with the layout of the publication, did little to help endear the collection's difficult and strikingly novel poetry to its first reading public, with only a handful of names, including Heine and Hegel, speaking out in favour of the collection.

Johann Wolfgang Goethe, West-Eastern Divan in Twelve Books, translated by Edward Dowden, edited by E.D.D. [Elizabeth Dickinson West Dowden], London 1914, Taylorian FIEDLER.J.1100, online

As Dickinson West reports in the preface to the volume, by the turn of the twentieth century the *Divan* was still very little known, both in England and in Germany. It was largely thanks to Germanists, such as Konrad Burdach, who laid the philological groundwork for subsequent *Divan* scholarship, writers, such as Hugo von Hoffmanstahl, and songs that the collection, or at least parts of it, reached a wider audience. The translation by Dowden, President of the English Goethe Society for 22 years, played an important role bringing the work to a broader, international audience at a time of turmoil. Movingly, his widow wrote in the foreword to the translation in December 1913 that Goethe 'turned to the East as to a refuge from the strife of tongues, as well as from the public strife of European swords'. The annotations to the text include the most recent research, for example consistently pointing out when poems such as 'Suleika' were authored by Marianne von Willemer while Goethe had included her poems without attribution in the *Buch Suleika*.

Autograph album for Cécile Mendelssohn Bartholdy, Bodleian Libraries, University of Oxford. MS. M. Deneke Mendelssohn b. 2

The album was given to Felix Mendelssohn Bartholdy's wife as Christmas present in 1844. On fol. 10r, Felix' sister Fanny Hensel wrote her setting of 'Suleika' with an illustration by her husband Wilhelm Hensel. The image was commissioned in 1836, but was for some reason removed and included in the 1844 book.

A New Divan: A Lyrical Dialogue between East & West, eds Barbara Schwepcke and Bill Swainson (London: Gingko 2019)
Taylorian PN6101 NEW 2019

Two centuries after its initial publication, and a century after Dawson's translation, the *Divan* occupies a significant place in world literature. It continues to challenge and inspire readers and students, engendering a range of artistic and cultural responses. Only a decade after the first English translation, the Urdu poet Muhammad Iqbal honoured the *Divan* in his *Payam-i-Mashriq* (1823). In our time, Edward Said and Daniel Barenboim named their orchestra for peace and dialogue after the collection. The *New Divan* follows in this spirit. The collection features 24 poetic commissions chiefly in Arabic, with some poems in German, Spanish, Italian, French, Russian, Slovenian, Turkish, Portuguese and Persian, together with English translation on facing pages, and six essays which 'discuss the challenges of literary and cultural translation' in the words of Barbara Schwepcke. It provides a fitting continuation of the *Divan* project that Goethe himself noted as 'unvollkommen' in 'Künftiger Divan'.

2.2. A World-Story of Tolerance

It is tempting to regard Goethe's *Divan* as uniquely advocating for an open-minded engagement with the 'foreign'. But in the *Noten und Abhandlungen*, the poet himself listed a number of figures whose work he consulted, among them Johann Gottfried Herder, Heinrich von Diez, and the afore-mentioned Hammer. Another important precursor to the *Divan*'s model of intercultural dialogue comes with Gotthold Ephraim Lessing's drama *Nathan der Weise*, which advocated for the Enlightenment ideal of toleration, encapsulated in the parable of the ring which Nathan tells the sultan Saladin.

Case 2.2: *Nathan der Weise* edition, translation and reception
Photograph Henrike Lähnemann

Gotthold Ephraim Lessing, *Nathan der Weise. Ein Dramatisches Gedicht, in fünf Aufzügen* [n.p.] 1779 (?), Taylorian ARCH.12°.G.1779
The Taylorian copy is one of three unauthorized editions with imprint date of the genuine first edition. The stamps on the title page and the bookplate on the flyleaf show that it once belonged to the Hamburg collector Adolf Glüenstein (1849-circa 1917) but was acquired from the library of the German-Jewish Germanist Friedrich Gundolf (1880–1931), a member of the George-Kreis. His habilitation on 'Shakespeare und der deutsche Geist' (1911) was a milestone in literary criticism and the Taylorian made sure that the illustrious provenance was documented in the volume. In 1964, the Deutsche Akademie für Sprache und Literatur founded the Friedrich-Gundolf-Preis for the intermediation of German culture in foreign countries, something also strongly promoted by Müller and Fiedler (Case 3).

Nathan the Wise. A dramatic poem, written originally in German by G.E. Lessing, printed 1791 in Norwich, published 1805 in London by R. Philips, Taylorian MONTGOMERY.7.F.3 & FIEDLER.J.3220.
The translation was undertaken and published as a political statement by William Taylor of Norwich, a business man who supported universal suffrage. He translated the "argumentative drama, written to inculcate mutual indulgence between religious sects", as he writes in the preface, in March 1790 "when questions of toleration were much afloat", and printed it for private distribution but "Now [1805] that the topic is acquiring a fresh interest, it has been thought fit that the remaining copies of that edition should be exposed to sale."

Angelika Overath, Navid Kermani, Robert Schindel, *Toleranz. 3 Lesarten zu Lessings Märchen vom Ring im Jahre 2003*, Göttingen 2010, Taylorian PT2399.T65 TOL 2010
The collection of essays arose out of a round table at the Herzog August Bibliothek in Wolfenbüttel. Together, the Austrian-Jewish poet Robert Schindel, the Orientalist Navid Kermani, and the German author Angelika Overath look at how to read the 'Ringparabel' in the 21st century.

Case 3: German in Oxford

Case 3: Friedrich Max Müller as image, as a lecturer on language, and as author translated into Korean and Arabic
Photograph Henrike Lähnemann

Since the foundation of the Taylorian, the Germans and Germanists working there (often in Personalunion) saw it as their mission to make German literature known not only to their students but also to a wider Oxford public and beyond. Notable figures from the early days include professors Friedrich Max Müller, Hermann Fiedler, and Siegbert Prawer. This has been continued right to the present day with many colleagues working as editors and translators, with a special focus on contemporary authors. A whole series of the 'Treasures of the Taylorian' (see Case 1) is dedicated to 'Writers in Residence' into which also activities by students are integrated. The work of the first (unofficial) 'Writer in Residence' at the Institution, Luisa Hewitt's *The Chronicle of Wisa Dingeldey by Herself*, is presented here.

3.1. Friedrich Max Müller: A Bestselling Oxford Germanist

The second professor for Modern European Languages at the Taylorian and renowned Sanskrit scholar Friedrich Max Müller was one of the key academic figures in Victorian Britain. His main interest was a comparative approach to language and religion, in a wide Indo-European perspective. The original manuscripts of several of his key publications are held at the Taylorian.

Photographic Print of Friedrich Max Müller (c. 1875)
    Taylorian MS 8° G. 76
Friedrich Max Müller, *On Language* (1891), autograph manuscript
    Taylorian MS 8° E 31.
Friedrich Max Müller *On Language*, in: Proceedings of the Philosophical Society of Glasgow, Glasgow 1891, Taylorian 4.C.27; Google Books

Müller landed a world-wide hit with his only novel, a romance entitled 'Deutsche Liebe' which for a while was the most read German book in places such as Korea. There are numerous English translations of it. The German edition with Brockhaus ran to over twenty editions before 1925 but then lost popularity. Müller uses his academic standing for the age-old device of presenting himself as the editor rather than as author of fragments of papers left to him by a stranger, headed as 'memories'. In the conversations between the protagonist and his love-interest, the disabled duchess, a wide range of European literature is discussed: Dante, Shakespeare, Rückert poems, Tennyson, Burns, Matthew Arnold, Carlyle's *Past and Present*; pages of extracts from Tauler in a special Gothic font are included. The duchess takes the stand of 14th cent. German mysticism with the protagonist countering with Luther's Protestant theology.

Deutsche Liebe. Aus den Papieren eines Fremdlings, Leipzig: Brockhaus 1857 (German first edition): Taylor Institution 35.K.13.A, on Google Books

Amour allemand. Souvenirs recueillis dans les notes d'un étranger, Paris 1873. Taylorian 35.K.13.B. The translator A.P. recounts having started the translation encouraged by the physicist Émile Verdet (1824–1886) directly after it was first published but then let it rest because of the political tension between Germany and France; the translation is dedicated to Verdet and 'l'illustre philologue d'Oxford, M. Max Müller' whom the translator believed to be just the editor. The Taylorian bookplate states: 'presented by the Publisher', Google Books

German Love. Fragments from the Papers of an Alien, translated from the 6th German edition by G.A.M. [Georgina Adelaide Müller], London: W. Swan Sonnenschein & Co. 1884, presented by Prof. T J [Jim] Reed in 2004; Taylorian TNR13421. Earlier translation in 1863 by J.M. in the Weston; later translation in 1898 by M.G.A., American edition 1905.

독일인의 사랑 (*Dogirinui sarang*), transl. into Korean by Kyung-ah Cha, Seoul: Literary Publishing House 2015. Taylorian, yet uncatalogued, donated by Prof. Juni Hoppe in April 2025 for the exhibition

Ibtisāmāt wa-dumūʿ ('Smiles and Tears'), transl. into Arabic by Mayy Ziyādah, ed. by Sīmūn ʿAwwād, Beirut: Mūʾassasat A. Badrān wa-Sharikāh [1973]. Dedication in translator's handwriting. Taylorian PF M3.4

3.2. Hermann Fiedler

Hermann Georg Fiedler (1862–1945) was Professor of German at Oxford from 1907 until his retirement in 1937. The Taylor Institution Library holds his archive, gradually improving descriptions of the contents, most recently of box MS 8° G. 56, labelled 'foreign correspondence'.

FIEDLER COLLECTION

Book plate of the Taylorian for the Fiedler Collection, Taylorian Fiedler.L.930

The Taylorian also received Fiedler's extensive collection of books, especially strong on holdings of Goethe. His book plate even featured the motto 'Mehr Licht', supposedly Goethe's last words.

Letter from Fiedler to the King, presenting his *Oxford Book of German Prose* in 1943 and Letter from the agent of Stefan George to Fiedler, both Taylorian MS. Fol. G.12. An article on the archive by Emma Huber, 'Networks, Exchanges and Cultural Transfer in the Inter-War Period: an Examination of Correspondence in the Archive of Professor H.G. Fiedler' is forthcoming in the volume *Forum for Modern Language Studies. Special Issue: Migration Collections: Translocation Research in Libraries and Archives, 1850–2025*, ed. by Sophia Buck and Stefanie Hundehege.

Oxford Book of German Prose / Das Oxforder Buch deutscher Prosa von Luther bis Rilke, ed. by H.G. Fiedler, Oxford 1943, Taylorian FIEDLER.P.271, Emma Huber 'H.G. Fiedler and German Studies' *OGS* 50/4 (2022)

Oxford Book of German Verse, ed. by Hermann Fiedler, Oxford 1933, dedication to Oscar Lemont, a refugee who did the bust of Fiedler 1940, Taylorian yet uncatalogued. A German pre-runner with a preface by Fiedler's friend Gerhard Hauptmann was *Das Oxforder Buch deutscher Dichtung vom 12ten bis zum 20sten Jahrhundert*, 1911

Fiedler used his editorial work as cultural diplomacy, sending his collection of German prose to the king whom he had taught German.

Faustus: from the German of Goethe, with illustrations by Moritz Retzsch, London 1821 (Fiedler.L.930), copy on Google Books.

The first English translation is more of a precis, commissioned by the publisher to explain the engravings by Retzsch, shortened since the 'immoral tendency of allusions' in the play would make the full text 'offensive to English readers'.

Book plate of Hermann Fiedler, Taylorian Fiedler.L.930
See the blog post 'Faust in Oxford' on Fiedler's large collection of Faust editions.

3.3. An Insider Account of Life in the German Library

At the end of the 19th century, a German-British girl grew up in the basement of the Taylorian: Luisa Hewitt, née Krebs, daughter of Heinrich Krebs who served as the second librarian at the Institution from 1871 to 1921. Later in her adult life, she turned her memories from that time into a *roman à clef*: In *The Chronicle of Wisa Dingeldey by Herself*, Hewitt offers a detailed account of how the library looked like at the turn of the century, from the basement and the Main Reading Room all the way up to the attic, and her descriptions feel strikingly familiar to today's visitors. The text is also not short of humorous anecdotes about her father who adhered to a strict daily routine and fulfilled his duties as a librarian with meticulous precision, yet was not fully aware of social protocol.

Simmon's copy of excerpts of *The Chronicle of Wisa Dingeldey by herself*, Taylorian MS. 8° E 43
The chapters typed up by Simmon's are those featuring the Taylorian which are also the ones published in the new edition.

Luisa Hewitt, The Girl Who Lived in the Library, ed. by Christina Ostermann (Treasures of the Taylorian: Series 2: Writers in Residence, vol. 5), 2025.

Case 4: The *Nibelungenlied* as German World

Nibelungenlied versions. Lecture notes by Friedrich Max Müller at the front
and by Hermann Fiedler at the back
Photograph Henrike Lähnemann

> *Wer nicht von dreytausend Jahren*
> *Sich weiss Rechenschaft zu geben,*
> *Bleib im Dunkeln unerfahren,*
> *Mag von Tag zu Tage leben.*
>
> Let him who fails to learn and mark
>   Three thousand years still stay
> Void of experience, in the dark,
>   And live from day to day.
>
> (Johann Wolfgang von Goethe,
> *West-östlicher Divan*, Stuttgart 1819, p. 97,
> *West-Eastern Divan*, Case 2, p. 74)

Travelling with 'German in the World' is not just a synchronic exercise, exploring the past can equally cross boundaries and discover literary inspiration in the otherness of previous periods. A pertinent example for German Studies is the world of the *Nibelungenlied* which has been, together with Goethe's Faust, the mainstay of German lecturing since the beginning of German as a university subject. It features in itself the epic and courtly world, ranging in geography from Xanten in the Netherlands to Hungary, linked by the journeys back and forth along the rivers Rhine and Danube. It also resonates particularly with the event bridging the AGS and the AGC (Anglo-German Colloquium for Medieval German Studies), 'Echoes and Voices of the Medieval in Contemporary Writing'. This features a conversation between Caroline Bergvall and Ulrike Draesner whose new version of the *Nibelungenlied* was launched 2016 in Oxford. Additional material on the rich topic of the *Nibelungenlied* in the Taylorian can be found in the exhibition catalogue which was conceived to complement a workshop on Homer and the *Nibelungenlied*; see the History of the Book blog.

Ulrike Draesner, *Nibelungen. Heimsuchung*, with illustrations by Carl Otto Czeschka, Stuttgart 2016, Taylorian PT2664.R324 N53 DRA 2016

Epic! Homer and the 'Nibelungen' in Translation, ed. by Mary Boyle, Philip Flacke, Timothy Powell, Oxford 2024 (Treasures of the Taylorian 3: Cultural Memory 7). Bodleian Offsite 751821251

Photographic reproduction of manuscript C of the *Nibelungenlied Chriemhilden Rache, und die Klage; zwey Heldengedichte aus dem schvvæbischen Zeitpuncte. Sammt Fragmenten aus dem Gedichte von den Nibelungen und aus dem Josaphat*, ed. Johann Jacob Bodmer (Zürich 1757), Taylorian ARCH.8°.G.1757

In the first modern edition of the *Nibelungenlied,* the text has undergone major changes. Bodmer cut about two thirds, presenting only the last part with the Burgundians at the court of Kriemhild's second husband Etzel and Kriemhild's revenge for the death of Siegfried together with 'fragments' from the first two thirds. This drastic interference with the text is part of an attempt to make it more like the *Iliad.*

Hermann Fiedler's notebook *Exzerpte,* Taylorian MS.8°.G.56(ii). box 1: notes for a lecture on the *Nibelungenlied*

Friedrich Max Müller, *Epic Literature und Niebelungen,* Taylorian MS 8° E 14 A

A strength of the Taylorian collections has always been a focus on working as closely as possible on the originals; the Taylorian collection of facsimiles, housed in one of the closed bookshelves on the gallery under the collective shelfmark ZA.556.GER, features a range of reproductions. The lecture notes by the first professors of German all reference manuscripts and early philological editions.

Margaret Armour, *The Fall of the Nibelungs*, illustrated and decorated by W.B. MacDougall, London 1897, Taylorian FIEDLER.G.600

Cyril W. Edwards, *The Nibelungenlied; the lay of the Nibelungs*, OUP 2010 Taylorian PT1579.A3 E38 NIB 2010

The two translations of the *Nibelungenlied* show different approaches taken in the 19th and 21st centuries. Armour tried to make it more accessible by including images drawn by her husband and based her text on existing modern German translations, in this case a parallel Middle and New High German text edition by Karl Simrock. The Oxford-educated Germanist Edwards took a more radical philological and foreignizing approach, highlighting the archaic otherness of the world of the medieval epic.

Case 5: Natasha A. Kelly

Books and installation photographs by Natasha A. Kelly
Photograph Santhia Velasco Kittlaus

Natasha A. Kelly's works invite the reader to a practice of learning what it means to be Black and German, rendering visible Black histories in past, present, and future. The avowed Afrofuturist and Black German feminist holds a doctorate in communication studies and sociology, and is an acclaimed author, editor, artist, curator, and mother. Kelly's artistic work has been presented at renowned venues such as Carnegie Hall in New York, the Goethe Theatre in Salvador de Bahia, and the German Historical Museum in Berlin. In 2018, her film debut *Milli's Awakening* was featured at the 10th Berlin Biennale. She has held teaching positions at various universities in Germany, Austria, and the United States, and is currently a Visiting Professor at the Berlin University of the Arts, as well as the founding director of Germany's first Institute for Black German Arts and Culture.

Kelly's works on display are a selection from numerous bestselling and longselling books, films, installations and scenic readings, centring around questions raised by Black German Feminism – and one's imagination evoked by them. They offer space for encounters that are yet to come.

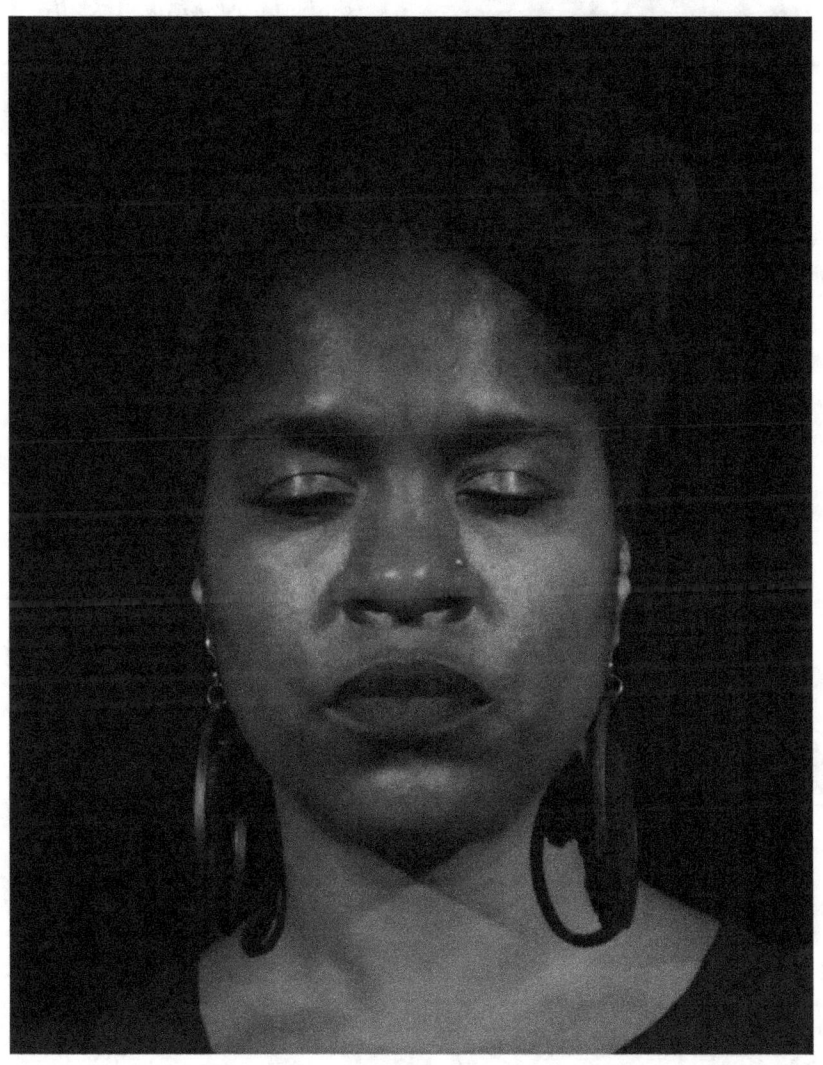

Film still of *Milli's Rising* (2019).
Credits: Natasha A. Kelly / Thabo Thindi

5.1. Books by Natasha A Kelly

Natasha A Kelly, *Schwarz - Deutsch - Weiblich : Warum Feminismus mehr als Geschlechtergerechtigkeit fordern muss.* München: Piper, 2023
Taylorian HQ1627 KEL 2024

Brings to light the blind spots of white Western feminism and invites us to learn from Kelly's Black feminist perspective about the multi-layered, structural entanglements of discrimination, racism, and gender inequality.

Natasha A Kelly, *Rassismus : Strukturelle Probleme brauchen strukturelle Lösungen!* (Zürich: Atrium Verlag, 2021).
Taylorian DD74 KEL 2021

Drawing on examples from recent debates, this publication explains why Germany is a country in denial about its structural racism and proposes a process-orientated approach that enables anti-racist activism aimed at changing the underlying systemic ideologies.

Mapping Black Europe : Monuments, Markers, Memories, ed. by Natasha A. Kelly, Olive Vassell (Bielefeld: Transcript, 2023).
Taylorian D212.2.B53 MAP 2023

Black communities have significantly shaped Europe's social and cultural landscapes, but their contributions remain largely unrecognized. In 'Mapping Black Europe', leading Black scholars and activists shed light on overlooked monuments, memorials, and narratives in major European capitals relevant to Black European history, introducing places and their communities.

Natasha A Kelly, *Afrokultur: "Der Raum zwischen gestern und morgen"* (Münster: Unrast, 2021).
Bodleian Offsite Storage: 309246539

In her dissertation, Kelly addresses colonial legacies in the supposedly 'objective' German knowledge production which dismisses Black knowledges in the context of German history. Through the examples of W. E. B. Du Bois, Audre Lorde and May Ayim, Kelly points the visionary way to a Black German historiography.

I am Milli : Ikonografien des Schwarzen Feminismus, curated by Natasha A. Kelly (Berlin: Orlanda, 2022).
Taylorian HQ1197 IAM 2022

This exhibition catalogue refers to the group exhibition I AM MILLI, curated by Kelly in 2022, in which eleven Black womxn present their agency through art, within the white German majority society, which has a habit of objectifying Black bodies.

Natasha A Kelly, *Millis Erwachen / Milli's Awakening: Schwarze Frauen, Kunst und Widerstand / Black Woman, Art and Resistance* (Berlin: Orlanda, 2019).
Bodleian Offsite Storage: 309246540

The bilingual publication accompanied the documentation of the same name commissioned by the 10th Berlin Biennale. For the title image see p. 15.

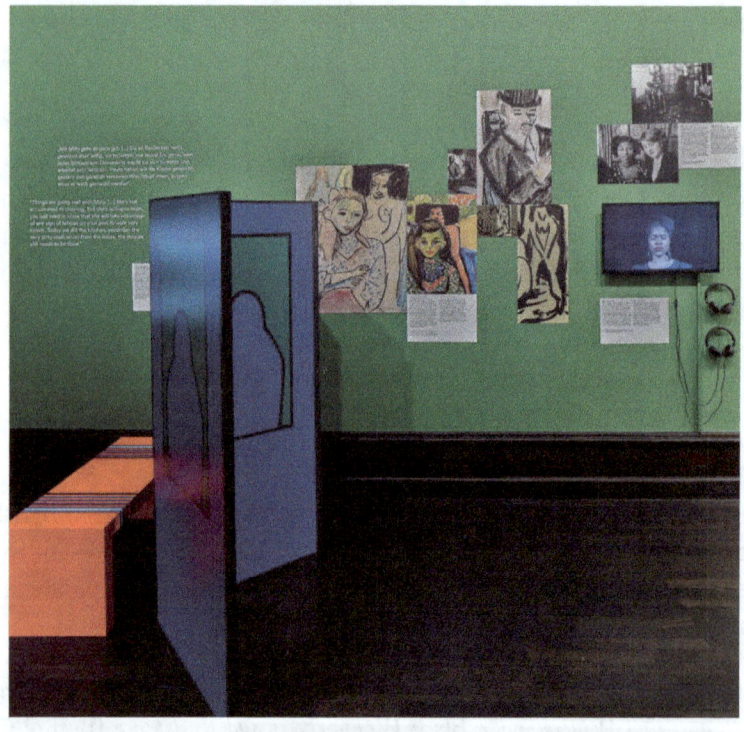

Installation *Wer war Milli?* (2022–2023) in the Kunsthalle Bremen
Credits: Marcus Meyer Photography

5.2. Installation and Theatre Images

Visual images form an important of Natasha A. Kelly's engagement with heritage and history. This exhibition case combines some of the striking film stills and installation photographs of her exhibitions.

Group exhibition 'I AM MILLI' (2022). Credits: Frank Gillich – see below.
Film 'Millis Erwachen / Milli's Awakening' (2018)
    Credits: Anh Trieu / Henning Fehr / Philipp Rühr – see p. 16.
Film 'Milli's Rising' (2019)
    Credits: Natasha A. Kelly / Thabo Thindi – see p. 76.
Installation 'Otto Müller Ausstellung' (2024)
    Credits: LWL MKuK / Hanna Neander – see below.
Installation 'Wer war Milli?' (2022-2023) in the Kunsthalle Bremen
    Credits: Marcus Meyer Photography – see p. 79.
Scenic reading 'Afrocultura' (Brazil 2019)
    Credits: Boccia Photos – see the cover of the book in Case 5.

Installation 'I AM MILLI' (2022)
Credits: Frank Gillich

www.ingramcontent.com/pod-product-compliance
Lightning Source LLC
Chambersburg PA
CBHW050343010526
44119CB00049B/680